LONGMAN CRITICAL ESSAYS

MEASURE FOR MEASURE

William Shakespeare

Editors:
Linda Cookson
Bryan Loughrey

Longman Critical Essays

Editors: Linda Cookson and Bryan Loughrey

Titles in the series:

CONTENTS

PREFACE

Like all professional groups, literary critics have developed their own specialised language. This is not necessarily a bad thing. Sometimes complex concepts can only be described in a terminology far removed from everyday speech. Academic jargon, however, creates an unnecessary barrier between the critic and the intelligent but less practised reader.

This danger is particularly acute where scholarly books and articles are re-packaged for a student audience. Critical anthologies, for example, often contain extracts from longer studies originally written for specialists. Deprived of their original context, these passages can puzzle and at times mislead. The essays in this volume, however, are all specially commissioned, self-contained works, written with the needs of students firmly in mind.

This is not to say that the contributors — all experienced critics and teachers — have in any way attempted to simplify the complexity of the issues with which they deal. On the contrary, they explore the central problems of the text from a variety of critical perspectives, reaching conclusions which are challenging and at times mutually contradictory.

They try, however, to present their arguments in a direct, accessible language and to work within the limitations of scope and length which students inevitably face. For this reason, essays are generally rather briefer than is the practice; they address quite specific topics; and, in line with examination requirements, they incorporate precise textual detail into the body of the discussion.

They offer, therefore, working examples of the kind of essay-writing skills which students themselves are expected to develop. Their diversity, however, should act as a reminder that in the field of literary studies there is no such thing as a 'model' answer. Good essays are the outcome of a creative engagement with literature, of sensitive, attentive reading and careful thought. We hope that those contained in this volume will encourage students to return to the most important starting point of all, the text itself, with renewed excitement and the determination to explore more fully their own critical responses.

How to use this volume

Obviously enough, you should start by reading the text in question. The one assumption that all the contributors make is that you are already familiar with this. It would be helpful, of course, to have read further — perhaps other works by the same author or by influential contemporaries. But we don't assume that you have yet had the opportunity to do this and any references to historical background or to other works of literature are explained.

You should, perhaps, have a few things to hand. It is always a good idea to keep a copy of the text nearby when reading critical studies. You will almost certainly want to consult it when checking the context of quotations or pausing to consider the validity of the critic's interpretation. You should also try to have access to a good dictionary, and ideally a copy of a dictionary of literary terms as well. The contributors have tried to avoid jargon and to express themselves clearly and directly. But inevitably there will be occasional words or phrases with which you are unfamiliar. Finally, we would encourage you to make notes, summarising not just the argument of each essay but also your own responses to what you have read. So keep a pencil and notebook at the ready.

Suitably equipped, the best thing to do is simply begin with whichever topic most interests you. We have deliberately organised each volume so that the essays may be read in any order. One consequence of this is that, for the sake of clarity and self-containment, there is occasionally a degree of overlap between essays. But at least you are not forced to follow one — fairly arbitrary — reading sequence.

Each essay is followed by brief 'Afterthoughts', designed to highlight points of critical interest. But remember, these are only there to remind you that it is *your* responsibility to question what you read. The essays printed here are not a series of 'model' answers to be slavishly imitated and in no way should they be regarded as anything other than a guide or stimulus for your own thinking. We hope for a critically involved response: 'That was interesting. But if *I* were tackling the topic . . . !'

Read the essays in this spirit and you'll pick up many of the skills of critical composition in the process. We have, however, tried to provide more explicit advice in 'A practical guide to essay writing'. You may find this helpful, but do not imagine it offers any magic formulas. The quality of your essays ultimately depends on the quality of your engagement with literary texts. We hope this volume spurs you on to read these with greater understanding and to explore your responses in greater depth.

A note on the text

All references are to the New Penguin Shakespeare edition of *Measure for Measure*, ed. J M Nosworthy.

Kim Reynolds

Kim Reynolds lectures in English at Roehampton Institute, and is the author of numerous critical studies.

ESSAY

Power and pleasure: *Measure for Measure*

In a recent article on playing The Duke in *Measure for Measure*, the actor Daniel Massey describes the play as very modern in its style and characterisation but problematically dated in its understanding and representation of the church and state, the institutions which are central to the action and meaning of the text. The problem arises, he says, because the functions of these institutions 'have changed so ineradicably since Shakespeare's time that they can seem almost inaccessible to us now.'[1] Massey's belief, one widely shared by critics and students of *Measure for Measure*, that we can no longer understand the nature of the institutions at the heart of the play because the passage of time has made them alien and incomprehensible, is misguided. The play is in fact making a very astute analysis of the way in which an essentially medieval form of government, in which a ruler's power was highly visible, concentrated in his/her person, and readily justified through constantly shifting political alliances, was adjusted in response to changing domestic and external

---

[1] D Massey, 'The Duke in *Measure for Measure*', ed. R Jackson, and R Smallwood, *Players of Shakespeare 2* (Cambridge, 1989), pp. 13–14.

situations to form the prototype of the political institutions we know today. It does so by enacting a situation in which the methods by which a ruler maintains his power change from the medieval to the modern, suggesting both how and why such a change came about. Thus, far from dealing with institutions unrecognisably different from our own, *Measure for Measure* tells us much about the ways in which contemporary institutions operate.

Look, for instance, at the dialogue which opens Act I scene 2:

> LUCIO If the Duke, with the other dukes, come not to composition with the King of Hungary, why then all the dukes fall upon the King.
>
> FIRST GENTLEMAN Heaven grant us its peace, but not the King of Hungary's!
>
> SECOND GENTLEMAN Amen.
>
> LUCIO Thou conclud'st like the sanctimonious pirate, that went to sea with the Ten Commandments, but scraped one out of the table.
>
> SECOND GENTLEMAN 'Thou shalt not steal'?
>
> LUCIO Ay, that he razed.
>
> FIRST GENTLEMAN Why, 'twas a commandment to command the captain and all the rest from their functions. They put forth to steal. There's not a soldier of us all that, in the thanksgiving before meat, do relish the petition well that prays for peace.
>
> SECOND GENTLEMAN I never heard any soldier dislike it.
>
> LUCIO I believe thee, for I think thou never wast where grace was said.
>
> SECOND GENTLEMAN No? A dozen times at least.
>
> FIRST GENTLEMAN What, in metre?
>
> LUCIO In any proportion, or in any language.
>
> FIRST GENTLEMAN I think, or in any religion.
>
> LUCIO Ay, why not? Grace is grace, despite of all controversy; as, for example, thou thyself art a wicked villain, despite of all grace.
>
> FIRST GENTLEMAN Well, there went but a pair of shears between us.

(I.2.1–28)

This is certainly not the the best-known scene in the play, but it is an important one. Those readers who pause over it generally consider the conversation as usefully fulfilling three functions. First, it establishes the debauched character of Viennese society. Second, it provides a sense of how the people are interpreting the Duke's absence. Finally, the war with Hungary to which Lucio refers is generally agreed to be analogous to England's war with Spain. In 1604, when Shakespeare is believed to have been writing *Measure for Measure*, King James was in the process of negotiating peace with Spain. The references in this passage can thus be understood to establish one of several parallels between Duke Vincentio and James I, and between the Vienna of the play and the London in which Shakespeare lived. The exchange has one other supremely important function: the references to the likelihood of imminent peace provide explanations for a great many of the problems posed by this play. Foremost among these is the overriding concern to control sexual behaviour — a concern so exaggerated that fornication is punished more severely than murder!

To understand the relationship between the coming of peace and the regulation of sexuality portrayed in this play it is useful to understand the ways in which sexuality has come to be used as an instrument of social control in modern Western societies. The French philosopher and critic Michael Foucault has written extensively about the connections between the regulation of sexual behaviour and the exercising of power by those in authority. In *The History of Sexuality*, Vol. 1, he attempts to identify how, when and why governments began to intervene in the sexual lives of their peoples. He concludes that the social changes which brought about the rise of the middle class, emphasis on individual achievement, and the celebration of the bourgeois nuclear family as a social and economic unit meant that there had to be similar changes in the ways in which those in authority maintained their power. The primary means of securing power and controlling the population ceased to be overt displays of might but became covert. People began to be coerced into giving their consent. Coercion operates through the dissemination of ideas and 'agreed' values to all levels of society, largely through the official institutions such as the church and the medical and legal professions. In order to coerce people effectively there has to be a system of collecting information about what people think, believe and do, and one of manipulating behaviour. The key to this kind of control is the defining and publicising of what is considered acceptable or 'normal' behaviour and what is suspect or 'abnormal'.

Such definitions were readily identified in relation to sexuality, making it a useful locus for control through coercion. Over time the religious, judicial, medical and psychiatric institutions all contributed to the definition of 'normal' sexual behaviour which has prevailed at least since the eighteenth century as that between heterosexual (preferably married) couples. As many people have shown, 'normal' sexuality in this sense has nothing to do with people's desires, instincts and practices and everything to do with what is useful for reproducing specific kinds of society. This attitude to acceptable sexual behaviour is relatively recent, and *Measure for Measure* seems to me to be fundamentally concerned with exploring the transition from a society characterised by a relatively open and tolerant attitude to sexuality to a recognisably modern one in which the state attempts to control and contain sexual activity. Accordingly, it looks at the nature of power, the machinery of repression, and the institutions which exist for collecting information.

According to Foucault, before the seventeenth century there *was* an official morality, but it was 'openly flouted, anatomies displayed and conjoined at will . . . bodies strutted about in their pride.'[2] It was a time when sexual language, sexual behaviour and all their implications were received with 'tolerant familiarity'.[3] This is a very good description of the Vienna we are shown at the beginning of the play. Act I scene 2 is set in a brothel where a number of 'gentlemen' have arranged to meet. It is portrayed as a regular meeting house, and they appear in this setting quite openly and unselfconsciously. The conversation of these young men is full of ribald jokes and graphic sexual observations which seem to characterise fashionable language:

---

[2] A Sheridan, *Michael Foucault: The Will to Truth* (London, 1980), p. 166.
[3] Sheridan, p. 166.

LUCIO   Behold, behold, where Madam Mitigation comes.

FIRST GENTLEMAN   I have purchased as many diseases under her
   roof as come to —

SECOND GENTLEMAN   To what, I pray?

LUCIO   Judge.

SECOND GENTLEMAN   To three thousand dolours a year.

FIRST GENTLEMAN   Ay, and more.

LUCIO   A French crown more.

FIRST GENTLEMAN   Thou art always figuring diseases in me, but
   thou art full of error. I am sound.

LUCIO   Nay, not, as one would say, healthy: but so sound as
   things that are hollow. Thy bones are hollow. Impiety has
   made a feast of thee.

(I.2.44–56)

This kind of dialogue may be natural in a brothel setting, but
the characters seem to feel no need to alter their style of address
in less appropriate situations. Lucio salutes Isabella at the
convent door, 'Hail, virgin, if you be . . .' (I.4.16). The interview
between Escalus, Pompey, Elbow and Froth (II.1) depends
entirely on *double entendre*, and Lucio's conversations with the
disguised Duke make no concessions to the fact that he is
supposed to be talking to a friar.

I would the Duke we talk of were returned again. This ungenitured agent will unpeople the province with continency. Sparrows
must not build in his house-eaves because they are lecherous.
The Duke yet would have dark deeds darkly answered. He
would never bring them to light. Would he were returned . . .
He's not past it yet, and I say to thee, he would mouth with a
beggar, though she smelt brown bread and garlic.

(III.2.162–173)

This unfettered attitude to sex has prevailed for at least fourteen
years and with the Duke's knowledge. Indeed, he himself admits
that his failure to enforce existing civil laws has amounted to
tacit consent to the people's behaviour.

So, why has the Duke decided to reactivate the legislation
governing sexual behaviour? He tells Friar Thomas that it is
because he has failed to enforce these laws for so long that:

> ... our decrees,
> Dead to infliction, to themselves are dead,
> And liberty plucks justice by the nose

> (I.3.27–29)

This clearly is an intolerable situation for if Vincentio is right, the relationship between ruler and ruled has been inverted:

> The baby beats the nurse, and quite athwart
> Goes all decorum.

> (I.3.30–31)

This is a partial explanation of why the Duke needs to reassert control over his people, but it doesn't tell us why he has chosen this particular moment, or why the regulation of sexual behaviour has become his primary concern. The answer to these questions is provided in the preceding scene (I.2). From the conversation between Lucio and his mercenary friends, it becomes apparent that the play is set in a period when the political situation is expected to shift from war to peace. War is often useful to those in power for it provides opportunities for propaganda and a means of uniting the population (think of the Falklands). What we see in *Measure for Measure* is the Duke deliberately replacing the soon to be defunct external threat with an internal bogey of his own devising: sexual licence. A redundant commander-in-chief defending the country against foreign invaders, he has created for himself a new role as defender of the social and moral fabric of the nation. His targets are the corruption, disease, and degeneracy he now sees as the consequences of promiscuity. What was once normal, natural behaviour has suddenly become abnormal, antisocial, and threatening.

This construction is articulated by Claudio who, though he resents his arrest still pronounces it to be just. He warns of the dangers of liberty. 'Liberty', he tells Lucio:

> As surfeit is the father of much fast,
> So every scope by the immoderate use
> Turns to restraint. Our natures do pursue,
> Like rats that ravin down their proper bane,
> A thirsty evil, and when we drink, we die.

> (I.2.125–129)

Significantly, Claudio does not refer to the effects of lechery but to liberty, which has more widespread social connotations, thus emphasising the subversive potential of unlicensed sexual activity.

The Duke decides that sexual behaviour must be visibly controlled and that it is desirable to avoid identifying the source of enforcement/repression as himself (the most recognisable single source of power in the state). He suggests that this is because he blames himself for the current situation, but the ways in which he disperses the source of control throughout society is significant for it prevents there being a single figure which could be resisted and suggests a general, shared attitude. He does this by absenting himself from the public eye and appointing not one, but two deputies. Then, disguised as a friar, he effectively disperses himself throughout the population, gathering information and covertly manipulating his subjects. In this way the Duke enacts what Foucault terms 'polyvalency', which means the exercise of power through presence at all levels of society. It is significant that the reader/audience is never allowed to forget the Duke's real power. We see him moving through all levels of society, ordering events to suit his own ends. This has two effects. First, it is reassuring and invites trust in the authority-figure. There is no chaos. We see the Duke pulling the strings and ensuring a happy ending. Second, and more importantly though less obviously, the way in which the Duke's machinations are consistently revealed comments on the nature of authority and questions the first feeling of trust. The operations of power, including the way in which those in authority seek to become invisible in order to disguise the nature and extent of their power, are made explicit. This activity is not necessarily condemned in the play, but, as always, Shakespeare reminds both the government and the people of the need to understand and monitor the power invested in the monarch.

In Angelo, Vincentio has chosen a figure who will never challenge his own popularity. He has chosen a surrogate who he knows will reactivate the laws that he now wants to be enforced and who will bear the brunt of public disapproval in his stead. Moreover, he engineers events so that he is not only welcomed back as the rightful ruler, but he is also able to demonstrate his own authority by revealing the truth of the situation and administering justice.

Significantly, the punishments on which the Duke finally decides publicly transform unofficial and unproductive relationship (for example, those which are outside wedlock and so produce illegitimate offspring) into productive ones (marriage and children able legally to inherit property). The emphasis on legal and productive unions is one which Foucault sees as the inevitable result of official intervention in sexual relationships. Marriage is useful to those in authority for it is an institution which is easily monitored and influenced. Through the official registration of marriages, births and deaths, the state is able to be kept informed about the whereabouts and activities of the people. Perhaps the most useful form of regulation which is associated with state advocacy of marriage is the way in which it embodies 'normal' sexual behaviour. Setting up social practices which encourage the reproduction of the existing power structure is the most effective means of control there can be. Ultimately individuals begin to regulate themselves to try to ensure that they conform to the norm. They also begin to resent, fear and seek to control those who deviate from it.

At the end of *Measure for Measure*, we see all of the unofficial relationships converted to official ones. It is important to note that each marriage comes about as the result of acknowledging and submitting to the Duke's authority. It is also necessary to be aware of two features about the marriages in this play. The first is that there is a definite shift in the kinds of marriages described at the beginning of the play and those enacted at its end. The first belong to a traditional model in which marriage is regarded primarily as about the making of alliances and the transfer of property. Such 'marriages of alliance' are consistently undermined in the course of the play: Mariana loses her dowry and so her husband; Juliet's dowry is in jeopardy because her relationship does not meet the alliance needs of her relations. According to Foucault, marriages of alliance began to be superceded by those based on sexuality in the late-eighteenth century. However, Shakespeare seems to anticipate this phenomenon in *Measure for Measure*. As well as undermining the claims of alliance marriages, he shows every match which the Duke seals in his final speech (including the one he proposes to Isabella) to be based entirely on sexual criteria.

The second distinctive feature about the marriages in this play is that, unusually for a Shakespeare play, marriage is not necessarily a reward for those involved but is presented more as a form of punishment. This might seem perverse as a form of propaganda for the institution of marriage, but the paradox is easily resolved. Foucault describes the relationship between the state (as source of repression) and sexuality as one which positively enhances sex by defining desire through its prohibitions and in the process adding an extra frisson: the fear of punishment.[4] This is a pleasure shared by those who exercise power (including the aspect of surveillance) and those who try to evade it.

This kind of relationship is readily identified in *Measure for Measure*. A good example is provided by Angelo's reactivation of the laws against sexual offenders and his reclamation of the 'red light' district of the city (a process Shakespeare observed for himself when, in September 1603, James I ordered that the property in the London suburbs inhabited by 'dissolute and idle persons' be demolished — ostensibly to help control the plague[5]). These measures require evasive action on the part of those who manage the brothels, and this is dramatised in the burlesque routine between Pompey, Elbow and Escalus in II.1. Pompey gives an account of the events which took place when Elbow's wife visited Mistress Overdone's new premises:

> Sir, she came in great with child, and longing — saving your honour's reverence — for stewed prunes. Sir, we had but two in the house, which at that very distant time stood, as it were, in a fruit dish, a dish of some threepence; your honours have seen such dishes; they are not china dishes, but very good dishes . . . having but two in the dish . . . Master Froth here, this very man, having eaten the rest . . . and . . . paying for them very honestly . . . [he was] cracking the stones of the foresaid prunes —
>
> (II.1.86–103)

---

[4] Sheridan, p. 175.
[5] The Arden Shakespeare, *Measure for Measure*, ed. J W Lever (London, 1965), p. xxxiii.

This speech relies for its humour largely on innuendo. Stewed prunes, cracking stones, and china dishes, for instance, all had familiar sexual connotations when the play was written.[6] Although the story is suggestive, it is nonetheless capable of a perfectly innocent interpretation. What it demonstrates is the shift in the language of sex from the open, explicit jokes and references at the beginning of the play to a more covert discourse. Pompey has not only learned to moderate his speech to suit his audience, but also proves adept at this game. By getting Escalus and the Justice to admit that they know the kinds of china dishes to which he refers, the tapster implies that they are at least familiar with the public rooms of establishments such as the one where he works.

Elbow, though the official tool of the authorities, can hardly be regarded as an agent of surveillance adept enough to make misleading him a pleasure. The Duke is the true collector of information. Disguised as a friar, he is even able to hear confessions (the confessional was one of the earliest and most effective means of collecting information and controlling behaviour; moreover, in this disguise the Duke visibly represents the two axes of the British sovereign's power — church and state). This ruse both supplies him with the special knowledge he needs to manipulate events and brings him into contact with every aspect of society: whores, pimps, fops, gentry, nuns, monks, officials, and governors. The result of his activities is not only the acquisition of knowledge about the private lives of his people, but also the generation of talk about sexual behaviour. The Duke/friar's conversations generally require the other speaker to discuss sexual matters. This illustrates yet another point identified by Foucault: that people often wrongly believe that a force repressing sexuality leads to silence on the subject. The opposite is in fact the case: as soon as the main avenue of discussion is blocked, an abundance of minor alternative but legitimate routes open up. Thus the effect of Angelo's attempts to control sexuality is to make people talk about it, and the Duke provides acceptable ways for them to do so.

---

[6] The Arden Shakespeare, p. 31.

My suggestion that the Duke's intention in going underground is part of a surveillance operation runs counter to a number of possible explanations for his actions. For instance, it has been suggested that Vincentio is a kind of Christ-figure who dons religious robes to go among the people and do good works. His return at the end of the play combines mercy and the attributes of a *deus ex machina*. There are certainly a number of biblical allusions and parallels in the text — not least that contained in the title, while quotes Matthew 7:2. While these references undeniably exist, such a reading of the play raises a battery of uncomfortable contradictions about characters' actions: why does Isabella seem to value her chastity more than Mariana's? Why does the Duke conceal the fact that he has saved Claudio's life? Why is Barnardine treated more leniently than Lucio?

A more satisfactory answer is that the Duke sports his monk's robe primarily to allow him access to his people's most private thoughts. This is exemplified in III.1 when the Provost conceals him so that he may observe what happens between Isabella and Claudio; indeed, his entire sojourn seems to be one of reconnaissance. He tells Friar Thomas that he wants to behold the effects of Angelo's actions and therefore disguises himself (I.3.42). Though no time limit was specified for the Duke's supposed absence, it was always known to be for a limited period, and throughout his professed transfer of power he had always the means to reclaim his authority at will. In fact, he exercises his power surreptitiously through the Provost to control events.

The final way in which I see Foucault's analysis of sexuality as a venue for exercising power being embodied in *Measure for Measure* deals with the problems posed by the unequal justice which seems to prevail in Vienna. The sentences imposed for sexual offences in the play vary enormously depending on the class of the offender. Claudio and Juliet, who belong to the leading class of society, are to be punished far more severely than Pompey and his associates. They all find themselves imprisoned, but only Claudio is threatened with death. Lucio, another gentleman, is the only offender who is denied total mercy at the Duke's hands. Even the murderer Barnardine is allowed to go free and seek to live a better life, but Lucio is forced to marry a prostitute by whom he has had a child. This is portrayed as the most serious punishment of all: the equivalent of 'pressing to death, whipping, and hanging' (V.1.519–520).

Why is Lucio so severely punished? The Duke says it is not for his slanderous speeches but for his promiscuous behaviour. Lucio presents the greatest obstruction to the institution of sexual control, and so needs to be the most vigorously controlled. Claudio and Juliet *want* a monogamous relationship. Angelo has only transgressed once, and this with a woman to whom he was legally contracted (though he did not know it at the time). Lucio, however, typifies those members of the upper classes who have participated fully in the sexual activities which prevailed at the opening of the play. According to Foucault, he is the natural scapegoat, for when sexuality came to be used repressively:

> The primary concern was not with the repression of the classes to be exploited, but rather the body, vigour, longevity, progeniture and descent of the classes that 'ruled'.

Sexual repression was thus a way of distinguishing between the classes to begin with and was only subsequently used to control the 'lower orders' once the ruling class was sufficiently protected by being believed to embody 'normal' behaviour.

The effectiveness of sexuality as a means of social control depends entirely on the fact that it is virtually impossible to control completely. There will always be transgressions and so the need for surveillance and a machinery of repression. This seems to me to account for the open ending of the play, for this is a play which is concluded rather than resolved. Traditionally marriages at the end of Shakespeare's plays are presented as essentially harmonious. They complete the action of the play, tie up loose ends, and restore the balance. In *Measure for Measure*, however, no such harmony exists. Each of the marriages begins by being slightly soiled, and the Duke's purpose in uniting the couples seems to be intended to create not a harmonious society (in which he would effectively be redundant), but one in which there is the potential for discord. This is precisely the kind of

---

[7] M Foucault, *The History of Sexuality*, vol. 1, trans. R Hurley (Harmondsworth, 1981), p. 123.

situation which needs controlling to keep it in order. Vincentio has used sexuality as a way of justifying his role and reaffirming his own power.

I have dealt here only with general issues surrounding sexuality, but the same approach can fruitfully be used to reveal specific practices within this general category. For instance, it would be interesting to consider the different kinds of controls exercised over men and women in the play, or the peculiarly patriarchal nature of sexual repression. The important point is that when *Measure for Measure* is read as a play which is intrinsically about documenting a historical moment when attitudes to sexuality were radically revised and reconstituted for political purposes, it ceases to be a 'problem play' and emerges as a sophisticated analysis of the ways in which those with power secure and maintain that power. The institutions it portrays are not moribund relics of a bygone age, but the original models for those which exist today. The questions we need to ask are not about the actions of the characters, but about the relationship between state power and sexual pleasure in *Measure for Measure*.

AFTERTHOUGHTS

1

Does Reynolds persuade you in this essay that imposing definitions of 'normal' sexual behaviour is a means by which those in
political authority retain their power?

2

What examples of 'polyvalency' (page 15) are you aware of in our
own social structures and political systems?

3

Do you agree with Reynolds's explanation as to why the Duke
disguises himself as a monk (page 19)? Does this affect your
view of his character and behaviour in any way?

4

Do you agree with Reynolds's interpretation of the 'open' ending
of the play (pages 20–21)?

Neil Taylor
*Neil Taylor is Dean of Arts and
Humanities at Roehampton Institute. He
is the author of numerous critical works.*

ESSAY

The title of
Measure for Measure

Of all the titles of Shakespeare's plays only *Measure for Measure*
is the proposition of an idea. In fact, it proposes a series of ideas,
for the title is a multiple pun. Among its many denotations and
connotations, the word 'measure' can lead us towards the worlds
of (*a*) religious discourse, (*b*) social control, (*c*) self-control,
(*d*) dancing, (*e*) sex. Let me explain.

(*a*) Jesus said, 'a good measure, pressed downe, shaken
together and running over shal men give into your bosome: for
with what measure ye mette, with the same shal men mette to
you again' (Luke 6:38, in the 1560 Geneva Bible translation).
This follows the famous statement, 'Judge not, and ye shal not
be judged'. The translators have here ensured once again that
the phrase is balanced, like a grocer's scales, with 'judge not' in
one scale and 'not . . . judged' in the other.

(*b*) The metaphor of the balance is highly appropriate,
embodying as it does the attitudes not only of the trader with his
scales, but the judge with the Scales of Justice. Thus we are
invited to think of not only the measurer with his rule but the
ruler with his measures. In the Old Testament, God is particularly associated with justice and punishment. Indeed, the
Duke's line 'An Angelo for Claudio, death for death!' (V.1.406) is

not only an embodiment of the Old Testament concept of an eye for an eye and a tooth for a tooth (Exodus 21:24), it also leads him two lines later into the formulation 'Measure still for Measure'. However, in the New Testament, Jesus talks of his Father's mercy and forgiveness. With these associations in mind, 'measure for measure' could mean 'balance Justice with Mercy, the Old Law with the New'.

(c) On the other hand, in a secular or more personal context, it could mean 'take a measured approach to life, avoid extremes, pursue the *via media*'.

(d) A measure is also a dance. The title of the play could mean 'dance for dance', or 'step for step'. In Shakespeare's late comedy *Pericles*, King Simonides throws a banquet at which Pericles, the Prince of Tyre, is an honoured guest. Simonides calls for music and dancing and bids Pericles join in:

> Come sir, here's a lady that wants breathing
> And I have heard you knights of Tyre
> Are excellent in making ladies trip,
> And that their *measures* are as excellent.

(II.3.100–104)

(e) In the quotation above, 'breathing' meaning exercise, but there is evidence that *th* and *d* were pronounced similarly in Elizabethan English, so it could also be a pun on 'breeding'. Furthermore, for the Elizabethans the dance was not only a profound metaphor for the essential harmony underpinning God's universe, it was also, in T S Eliot's phrase:

> The association of man and woman
> In daunsinge, signifying matrimonie —
> A dignified and commodious sacrament

> (*Four Quartets*, 'East Coker', part I)

The dance that celebrates wedding and the marriage-night is the stage emblem that almost always completes the kind of comedy that Shakespeare tended to compose.

Dancing may suggest marriage, but it is also 'suggestive', signifying sexual intercourse. Thus it is that Simonides puns on 'measure' ('I have heard your measures are excellent') punning on both 'penis' and 'vagina' — measure for measure.

Measure for Measure is, indeed, concerned with topics covered by *a* to *e* above — topics such as the nature of social justice, the importance of sexual morality, the implications of comedy, and the ultimate relationship of life to death.

1

A further way of thinking of the phrase 'measure for measure' is to see it as the formulation of an act of *exchange* or *substitution*. The image of someone pressing matter down, shaking it together and producing 'good measure' is easily applicable to a trader measuring out produce for sale and exchange. Trade is the substitution of one measure of one commodity for another measure of another commodity. In a barter society, the commodities might be, say, grain and fuel. In a society like our own, one might be grain but the other would always be money. Money is our medium of exchange, the item which we have come to prize above all other commodities because of its universal ability to provide a unit of substitution.

One can think of the whole art of Shakespeare's playmaking as a series of acts of substitution. First, there is the substitution of the fictional world of the play for the real world we inhabit, and therefore of the characters' identities for the actors' identities. Then there is the play's plot, which almost always involves acts of substitution too.

Measure for Measure begins with an act of substitution. Angelo is substituted for Vincentio. Vincentio tells Angelo 'be thou at full ourself' (I.1.43). But Vincentio conceives of the role of being Duke as itself an acting role, and his reluctance to be Duke any longer as the result of a recognition that 'I love the people,/ But do not like to stage me to their eyes' (I.1.67–68). So we already have a series of substitutions — Vincentio the actor substitutes another identity for his own, but dislikes his new identity and decides to ensure that a substitute takes it on instead.

2

The substitution of Angelo for Vincentio seems to involve the termination of one reign in order to make way for the next. Under normal circumstances this would only happen when the ruler dies. It would not be too far-fetched, therefore, to regard the play as beginning with a kind of death. From this point on the action of the play seems to be leading to another death, Claudio's. This does not, in the end, occur, but the avoidance of the dark consequences of the initial substitution is only achieved through a deed of darkness — the common device of Elizabethan drama (there are twenty-one examples) known as the 'bed trick'. And the bed trick is an act of substitution, in this case of Mariana for Isabella.

It could be argued that Shakespearean comedy is ultimately concerned with sex and Shakespearean tragedy is ultimately concerned with death. *Measure for Measure* has all the elements we would expect from a comedy. Those who are lost are found — Vienna is reunited with its lost Duke, Mariana with Angelo, Claudio with Juliet, Isabella with Claudio — and, like so many of Shakespeare's comedies, the play ends with a multiple marriage — Lucio is obliged to make up fourth place alongside Claudio, Angelo and the Duke. The new order of Vincentio's second term of office is celebrated in the pairing off, measure for measure, of eight sexual partners.

Balancing the play's concern with procreation, however, there is a remarkably sustained concern with dying. No Shakespeare play uses the word 'life' more often. On the other hand, I have counted over a hundred verbal allusions to death, and the words 'die' and 'died' both occur more often than in any other of Shakespeare's plays. If we look at the nature of the incidents making up the plot there is a similar balance of forces. Isabella's father is dead, so are eight of Mistress Overdone's husbands. Ragozine is dead and we see his head to prove it. The gallows stand in the background. Abhorson and Barnardine and Claudio are condemned to die. In the other scale are the three women 'with child' (Juliet, Mrs Elbow and Kate Keepdown) and the quadruple marriage which will follow the end of the play.

What the play has to say about death seems, for a long time, to be unsatisfactory. Many of its statements rehearse conventional paradoxes: death is the object of life's pilgrimage (II.1.36), it is sleep (II.2.90), it is the source of life (III.1.42). Sometimes the imagery of death creates a disturbed feeling-response. When Isabella talks of Claudio's impending death there is a cruel ambiguity in her opening phrase:

> He's not prepared for death. Even for our kitchens
> We kill the fowl of season. Shall we serve heaven
> With less respect than we do minister
> To our gross selves?

(II.2.84–87)

The idea that a man can prepare himself for death is contradicted by the idea that he gets prepared as a chicken does for the table.

Disturbing too is the way in which death and sex are sometimes very closely associated. Even if we don't go along with those critics who believe that Shakespeare treats decapitation as a form of castration and, therefore, an appropriate punishment for Claudio's sexual 'crime', there can be no doubt that both he and Isabella associate death with sexuality. There are other critics who see sexual repression reflected in the complicated thinking and feeling of the image in which she substitutes the deathbed for the lovers' bed:

> Th'impression of keen whips I'd wear as rubies,
> And strip myself to death as to a bed
> That long I have been sick for, ere I'd yield
> My body up to shame.

(II.4.101–104)

By comparison Claudio, who has a knowledge which his sister lacks, is direct and almost innocent in his assertion that:

> If I must die,
> I will encounter darkness as a bride,
> And hug it in mine arms.

(III.1.86–88)

Death is darkness, death is a sexual partner, death is 'it'. This image, of course, looks forward to the bed-trick, where identity is lost in sexual union in the dark. Death is a great disguiser.

For all the play's insistence on the idea of dying, death itself is implied rather than presented, and it is obscured or even evaded more than it is implied. In Act III scene 1, the Duke comes to Claudio in the disguise of a friar to prepare him for death. But the nature of death has to be inferred from what he says, since his speech concentrates on a description of life. There is just one extended statement about death, Claudio's famous speech, 'Ay, but to die, and go we know not where' (III.1.121–135). Even here, all we learn of death is that a dead body lies inert, cold and rotting, and then it turns to earth. The bulk of what Claudio has to say is not about death at all but about violent features of life — we are asked to imagine a victim of torture being 'kneaded', pressed and punched, then exposed to extremes of heat and cold, thrown into a cell, assaulted and deprived of rest, finally strung up 'pendent', howling in pain and terror. It is as if the most deathly image provided by the play is Vienna itself, an unreal city, corrupt in its incoherence. Elements of life abound, the fever of life and even, in Barnardine's commitment to not dying, a nobility, but Viennese sensibility is a perverted one in which death overbears life and truth is driven into dark corners.

Before coherence can emerge, something lost has to be found — the coherence which will satisfactorily define the relationship of body to spirit, mortality to immortality, and death to life. For most of the action, *Measure for Measure* is a murder mystery in which the corpse has gone missing. Not only that, but the murder has yet to be committed.

3

So who needs to be murdered? A father.

In many ways, *Measure for Measure* follows the pattern of 'new comedy' (a phrase which scholars use to describe the plays of the Roman dramatists, Plautus and Terence). In a typical 'new comedy', a young man wants to marry a young woman but his father opposes the marriage. However, a clever slave succeeds in outwitting the father and bringing about the marriage. In Shakespeare's treatment of the formula, Claudio and Juliet are the young couple, but they have already got beyond marriage in all but a literal sense before the play begins. On the other hand, Isabella and the Duke emerge as another pair of young lovers by the end of the play.

Who, then, is the father? Angelo is the best candidate, for he is the one who attempts to come between Claudio and Juliet. Yet Angelo is Vincentio's substitute. His significance is therefore largely determined by Vincentio's significance. Vincentio associates himself with 'fond fathers' (I.3.23) and, as Duke of Vienna, he is the father of his people. With Isabella, Claudio and Mariana, he is protective, caring and paternal. He is in disguise, but the guise is that of a father, a 'ghostly father' (IV.3.46). So, when Angelo becomes Vincentio's deputy, he thereby adopts the identity of a father. By temperament and by commission, Angelo acts like God the Father of the Old Testament, whereas Vincentio acts like the forgiving God the Father of the New Testament.

And who is the witty slave? Who ensures the happy outcome for Claudio·and Juliet? It has to be that bald-pated, lying rascal Friar Lodowick.

Thus Vincentio turns out to be playing *all* the male roles in new comedy — young lover, father, witty slave.

In romance, union grows to disunion and then to reunion. Siblings, lovers, friends, husband and wife, parent and child — one or other couple is parted, undergo trials and adventures, and find each other again. In *Measure for Measure* the pattern is there but, once again, distorted. Isabella and Claudio, the siblings, are parted as they go to separate cells, she to what she hopes is the strict restraint of Saint Clare's convent (I.4.4–5), he to prison (I.4.25). Moral disagreement threatens to intensify their divorce in III.1, and Claudio's execution would finish the job. The lovers who are also virtually husband and wife, Claudio and Juliet, are similarly separated by his entry into prison. Another pair of lovers, Angelo and Mariana, were separated by a typical romance agent, a storm at sea (which simultaneously separated a brother and sister), and they are further divorced by Angelo's perfidy. During these separations death threatens each of the men involved, and Claudio's spiritual trial, the dark night of a soul imagining death, is vivid enough to serve for all the others, and us as well. Act V brings the reunions, brother with sister, lover with lover, father with mother. But one relationship containable within the romance formula is missing, and that is parent with child.

One school of literary critics argues from anthropological studies of primitive nature rituals that, embedded in much of the narrative material which finds its way into literary texts, is a representation of an annual struggle between winter and spring, the Old Year with the New Year. It expresses itself often in stories telling of the killing of an impotent king, or the curing of his sickness, by a potent representative of youth. The story of Oedipus, for example, tells both of the killing of a king (his father) and of a youth curing sickness (Oedipus saves his father's city from plague). *Measure for Measure* provides us with a text which can be read in the light of such a theory too. The impotent old king's role is divided between Vincentio and Angelo. Angelo's blood is snow broth, his urine is congealed ice and, in Lucio's opinion, he is ungenitured. Vincentio has 'a purpose/ More grave and wrinkled than the aims and ends/ Of burning youth' (I.3.4–6) and he therefore adopts the guise of celibacy. The burning youth of Isabella brings Angelo to the point of death. Vincentio, however, sacrifices Angelo to his own rejuvenation as he woos Isabella for himself. Vincentio thus plays the Old Year and the New.

Another, very different, reading of the Oedipus story might point out the way in which Oedipus, by marrying his mother, creates a whole new network of relationships for himself, starting with an act of incest. By marrying his own mother, Oedipus becomes his own father. In *Measure for Measure*, Isabella's horror that Claudio might accept her sleeping with Angelo is expressed in the most extreme and perverse terms:

> Is't not a kind of *incest* to take life
> From thine own sister's shame?
>
> (III.1.142–143, author's italics)

Can she mean that Claudio is sleeping with his own sister? 'To take life' seems at first to be an accusation of murder, and she, as well as Angelo, certainly shows a willingness to equate loss of virginity with loss of life. But it must actually mean 'gain life', i.e. be born. This makes Isabella his mother, and the incest that between mother and son, Jocasta and Oedipus.

But the plot of *Measure for Measure* rests upon substitution.

Angelo is substituted for Vincentio at the beginning, and Mariana for Isabella at the end. If we allow the substitutions their own potency, Isabella would be committing incest with her own father if she consented to sleep with Angelo.

There are no actual parent-child relations in the cast list. We hear about fathers but they are dead (Isabella and Claudio's and, presumably, Mariana's). Claudio and Lucio have not married the mothers of their children. What the play lacks are real fathers and therefore observable liberating deaths. A whole generation is missing and must be found and then killed. The imagery of death thus continues to assert and, simultaneously, to evade the fact of death. The old are *ghostly* fathers thwarting and threatening to kill the young. When Angelo woos Isabella she, and we, must read it as incest. Only when he has been prepared to die is he released into his own generation and allowed to become a suitable lover for the 'Isabella' he has bedded, Mariana.

The bed-trick, by substituting Mariana for Isabella, implicitly enacts the relationship resulting from the substitution of Angelo for Vincentio. And Isabella's silence at the end of the play must result from her recognising the incestuous relationship she is being offered.

4

Vincentio is *not* offering incest. And if we ever felt he was — misunderstanding him, for example, when he called Isabella 'sister' (III.1.155) or 'daughter' (IV.3.116), or when she called him 'father' (3.1.239) — then the sign-language of drama tells us that he is not. At V.1.351 the ritual killing of a king is undertaken by Lucio. It is he, of all people, who performs the *coup de grâce* and the *coup de théâtre* when:

> He pulls off the Friar's hood, and discovers the Duke.

In order that the Father of Vienna can offer the play's final exchange, 'What's mine is yours and what is yours is mine' (V.1.534), the 'killing' of a 'father', through the substitution of Vincentio for Lodowick, proves to be the necessary measure.

AFTERTHOUGHTS

1

Do you consider that the connotations of 'measure' listed as *(a)* to *(e)* on pages 23–24 are all equally relevant to the play?

2

Explain Taylor's theory that 'For most of the action, *Measure for Measure* is a murder mystery in which the corpse has gone missing' (page 28). Are you convinced?

3

Is it reasonable to describe Isabella and the Duke as 'another pair of young lovers by the end of the play' (page 29)?

4

Explain the relevance to this essay of the discussion of the Oedipus story (pages 30–31).

Cedric Watts

Cedric Watts is Professor of English at Sussex University, and the author of many scholarly publications.

ESSAY

Why Barnardine?

In the plot-structure of *Measure for Measure*, Barnardine is redundant. If we had to re-write the plot of the play to make it tidy and efficient, Barnardine could be simply cut out. In this essay, therefore, I ask why Shakespeare bothered to include him at all.

1

So high is Shakespeare's prestige that many critics are inclined to argue that if something is present in a Shakespearian text, it must be there for a good reason. I have doubts. Given the discrepancies between the earliest surviving texts of many of his plays, it is quite likely that some of the material we now encounter may represent 'first thoughts', or notions that might have been discarded at some later stage. Shakespeare did not supervise the printing of his plays; had he done so, he might well have made substantial alterations for the occasion. Some characters might have been excised entirely.

One obvious example of a redundant character is the Clown in *Othello*. When I ask students what they think of that Clown, they sometimes reply on these lines: '*Is* there one? I don't recall one.' The Clown appears in Act III scene 1 and Act III scene 4 of *Othello*, but he is often omitted from productions on stage and screen; and I doubt that anyone has every complained about the omission. In III.1.1–30 he delivers a few feeble jests, including a coarse joke about wind-instruments; and in III.4.1–18 he puns unoriginally on 'lie' (meaning both 'reside' and 'tell a falsehood'). Quite probably the Clown's part was added merely to provide some work for the company's comic actor. The old romantic idea that a Shakespeare play is an 'organic whole', in which everything has its natural and rightful place, does not tally with the substantial evidence of textual corruption, revision, duplication and inconsistency which scholars (studying the early Quartos and Folios of the works) have so abundantly adduced.

In *Measure for Measure*, Barnardine at first appears to have an obvious function in the plot. His function is to provide a head — his own — to be substituted for Claudio's. The Duke, disguised as friar, is confident (in IV.2.89–110) that Angelo, having sated his lust, will consequently send a reprieve for Claudio. Angelo's letter, however, far from constituting a reprieve, orders the Provost to execute Claudio promptly and to send the victim's head to Angelo as proof. The 'friar' must therefore rapidly improvise a new scheme to save Claudio: Barnardine must be speedily executed and his head substituted for Claudio's. In the event, however, when the 'friar' calls on Barnardine to submit to execution, that reprobate stubbornly declines to cooperate: 'I swear I will not die today for any man's persuasion.' What is to be done? The Provost then reveals a providential coincidence:

> Here in the prison, father,
> There died this morning of a cruel fever
> One Ragozine, a most notorious pirate,
> A man of Claudio's years, his beard and head
> Just of his colour. What if we do omit
> This reprobate till he were well inclined,
> And satisfy the deputy with the visage
> Of Ragozine, more like to Claudio?

(IV.3.67–74)

The Duke piously comments, 'O, 'tis an accident that heaven provides'; and sophisticated theatregoers are likely to chuckle inwardly at this blatant use of coincidence to rescue the plot from an impasse. Of course, Ragozine's head is sent to Angelo and does indeed fool him into thinking that Claudio has been executed. Thus, anyone who values neat plot-construction will see that the original problem, that of finding a portable head, has been solved by the convenient death of Ragozine, and has rendered superfluous the introduction of Barnardine. Shakespeare got matters right the second time, but should have tidied the story by eliminating Barnardine entirely; or so it might be said. A counter-argument follows.

2

In Act III of the play, the 'friar'/Duke emerges vigorously as a benevolent schemer who, by his stratagems, hopes to right the wrongs being inflicted by Angelo. If dramatic suspense is to be maintained, it will depend largely on our sense that the 'friar'/Duke, though so confident, is fallible and capable of making miscalculations. We have noted that by failing to anticipate Angelo's perfidy, he completely misjudges the deputy's likely response to the 'bed-trick' (when Angelo thinks he has copulated with Isabella). He also miscalculates rather naïvely when assuming that Barnardine will readily collaborate in his own execution. 'Call your executioner, and off with Barnardine's head,' says the 'friar' briskly to the Provost; 'I will give him a present shrift and advise him for a better place' (IV.2.199–201). Barnardine, however, is adamant: 'Friar, not I. I have been drinking hard all night and I will have more time to prepare me, or they shall beat out my brains with billets' (IV.3.51–53). A drunken man is indeed in no state to make the act of contrition which should (in Catholic liturgy) precede death. So, for a while, the 'friar'/Duke is baffled; and this has large critical consequences.

Various influential critics, including G Wilson Knight, Nevill Coghill and F R Leavis, have seen the Duke as a fully authoritative and trustworthy pillar of virtue. Here is Wilson Knight:

> The Duke, lord of this play in the exact sense that Prospero is

lord of *The Tempest*, is the prophet of an enlightened ethic. He controls the action from start to finish, he allots, as it were, praise and blame, he is lit at moments with divine suggestion comparable with his almost divine power of fore-knowledge, and control, and wisdom . . . Like Prospero, the Duke tends to assume proportions evidently divine . . . The Duke's ethical attitude is exactly correspondent with Jesus's . . . the Duke is, within the dramatic universe, automatically comparable with Divinity.[1]

So the Duke is supposed to be virtually God on earth, imparting with supreme authority and 'fore-knowledge' the New Testament doctrine of love and mercy. (The critic seems to have forgotten that unmerciful Duke who says 'Call your executioner, and off with Barnardine's head' (IV.2.199–200).) Nevill Coghill subsequently supported this Christian interpretation.[2] F R Leavis commended Wilson Knight's view, claiming that the Duke should be seen as 'a kind of Providence directing the action from above'; and he echoed Knight's phrasing in declaring:

> The nature of the action as a controlled experiment with the Duke in charge of the controls, has asserted itself sufficiently.

How should we regard Barnardine?

> . . . towards him we are left in no doubt about the attitude we are to take: 'Unfit to live or die', says the Duke, voicing the general contempt.[3]

It seems to elude Leavis's awareness that the encounter between the Duke and Barnardine may reasonably cause some contempt to be directed against the Duke himself. Leavis suggests that one thematic function of Barnardine is to illustrate the life-denying nullity of the stoical philosophy commended by the 'friar' at III.1.5–41. But in that case, it could be argued that the rather callous duplicity of the Duke is revealed, for in that speech he purported to be a friar offering sound

---

[1] G Wilson Knight, *The Wheel of Fire* (originally published in 1930) (London, 1960), pp. 74, 79, 82.
[2] See Nevill Coghill, 'Comic Form in *Measure for Measure*', *Shakespeare Survey* 8 (1955).
[3] F R Leavis, *The Common Pursuit* (1952) (Harmondsworth, 1962), pp. 170, 164.

religious consolation (and he readily let Claudio believe that death was imminent, even though he intended to save him). The fruitless encounter with Barnardine is just one of numerous instances of the Duke's fallibility. Far from being a virtually divine omniscience conducting a 'controlled experiment', this Duke is all too human in his proud belief that he should manipulate others for their own good. Barnardine's stubborn refusal to be manipulated calls in question that 'almost divine power of fore-knowledge' which Wilson Knight had attributed to him. Instead of illustrating his authority as a fount of Christian moral wisdom, the Duke's futile alacrity in seeking to execute Barnardine may remind us of the wide variety of morally suspect actions that may be attributed to him.

The list of those actions is extensive. In the first place, the Duke shows a combination of laxity and cowardice. As he concedes, it was he who, through lax rule, let corruption become widespread, so that 'liberty plucks justice by the nose'. He then displays cowardice in appointing Angelo to restore order, instead of shouldering the responsibility himself. Furthermore, with bewildering illogicality, he says he has appointed Angelo in order to discover whether Angelo is as good as he seems. (If he doubted Angelo's integrity, he should not have entrusted to him a crucially important task.) Angelo does not have a free hand; he is obliged to enforce the laws, and the Duke has left him instructions. Yet those laws, for which the Duke is ultimately responsible, seem crazily severe, since lovers who are effectually married (but whose marriage has not been ratified in a religious ceremony) can be sentenced to death for copulation. At the end of the play, the Duke pronounces public justice which eventually appears generously lenient; but the old problem remains. The problem was that of changing the laws to make them just, fair and discriminating. The Duke's personal acts of clemency may undo the damage (for much of which he himself was ultimately responsible), but they do not constitute a legislative basis for social justice. In a less realistic comedy, the 'poetic justice' of this dénouement would be far less problematic; but, as *Measure for Measure* has offered so vivid and cogent a presentation of problems of social justice and public morality, we are led to give particularly searching attention to the solutions that seem to be provided. So the confrontation between the Duke and Barnardine is part of that sequence of events in which a critical sub-text seems to be challenging the dominant text. If the dominant text seems to support autocratic authority, the sub-text sharply questions it. (The reader's political prejudices may become evident: left-wing readers predictably tend to give more emphasis to that questioning.)

When the 'friar'/Duke first enquires about Barnardine, who is due 'to be executed in th'afternoon', the Provost remarks that Barnardine has been languishing in jail for 'nine years'. The 'friar'/Duke's response is remarkable:

> How came it that the absent Duke had not either delivered him up to his liberty or executed him? I have heard it was ever his manner to do so.
>
> (IV.2.129–31)

The first remarkable point is that the Duke seems to be unaware of what goes on in his own jail. Once again, critics who believe that the Duke 'has an almost divine power of fore-knowledge' overlook the extent to which the ruler of this state needs to learn a great deal about his own limitations. In the past, he has been too reclusive:

> ... I have ever loved the life removed,
> And held in idle price to haunt assemblies
>
> (I.3.8–9)

He has failed to keep in touch with the people; so it serves him right that Lucio propagates such gross (and entertaining) slanders about 'the old fantastical Duke of dark corners' (IV.3.155–156) who 'would mouth with a beggar, though she smelt brown bread and garlic' (III.2.172–173). By the end of the play, the Duke has changed (though he would be more sympathetic had he candidly acknowledged the extent of the change): he has come to know the people at first hand, and he is now prepared to let justice be done in the open street, in a public forum. Again, at the beginning of the play, he scorned love, deeming himself superior to such trifling matters:

> Believe not that the dribbling dart of love
> Can pierce a complete bosom.
>
> (I.3.2–3)

In the last Act, however, he offers his hand in marriage to Isabella; so he has come to recognise that his 'bosom' was not as 'complete' as he once thought. (Whether she accepts his offer, as used to be assumed, or rejects it, as Jonathan Miller suggested, is a matter of directorial judgement.[4] The text seems to me to support — but in a peculiarly reticent, unenthusiastic way — the former outcome.)

The revelation by the 'friar' that the Duke either freed or executed the prisoners exposes a bizarrely crude and arbitrary procedure; common sense suggests that there should be a wide range of intermediate options. His polarisation of justice (one pole being the severity of capital punishment, the other being the laxity of free pardon for culprits) reflects what is wrong in the legal system of the state as a whole, for its laws — as Claudio and Juliet have found — lack discriminating selectivity. When the 'friar'/Duke calls on Barnardine to prepare for death, the 'friar' is tellingly aligned with the grotesque executioner, Abhorson, and with the cynical pimp, Pompey (now serving the state as executioner's assistant); so, in this tableau on stage, the authority of the state looks distinctly tarnished, and the audience's sympathies are likely to flow strongly towards Barnardine. Leavis claimed that we should feel not sympathy but contempt for him, as one 'unfit to live or die'. This is not the effect created in stage productions that I have seen. One's sympathies tend naturally to be evoked by the outnumbered underdog. Barnardine's first appearance in the play is brief but forceful; he makes his mark. He provides a cameo-role for a vigorous actor, because in a few lines he strongly establishes his own character: distinctive, stubborn, impenitent, hung-over, yet proudly defiant.

A central theme in the play is that of death (its nature, and how we should prepare for it) and the death-sentence. In its treatment of capital punishment, *Measure for Measure* seems liberal and progressive, far in advance of orthodox thought in Shakespeare's day. In the treatment of Claudio (who veers between stoicism and a desperate desire to live), Shakespeare

---

[4] In Jonathan Miller's production at the Greenwich Theatre (London, 1975), Isabella recoiled in silent horror from the Duke's proposal.

offers what is now a familiar, but very strong, argument against capital punishment: the wrong person may suffer irrevocably. In the treatment of the recalcitrant Barnardine, Shakespeare offers a different argument. Even if a person is rightly found guilty of a crime which, in law, merits capital punishment, could you really — if you were face to face with that person — decree his instant death? What the Duke's confrontation with Barnardine suggests is that it is easy to be severe with people whom we do not really know; if we were to meet them face to face and learn of their distinctive personalities, we might find severity less easy. Barnardine's 'stubborn soul' defeats the Duke's manipulative zeal; and, eventually, he is reprieved and freed.

To conclude. If the criterion is neat and tidy plot-construction, Barnardine is redundant. If the criterion is the effective dramatic exploration of moral, judicial and political problems, Barnardine's presence is amply justified. Shakespeare contorts the plot to develop the themes of this superbly dialectical and contrastive play. A relatively superficial reading of the text may suggest that the Duke is a benevolent 'white Machiavel' whose schemes, justified by the knowledge of human nature that they elicit, culminate in a handsome dispensation of lenient justice. A more attentive reading reveals a potent and detailed questioning of autocratic authority; social justice, it seems, is too important to be entrusted to autocrats, however benevolent they may purport to be. In the play's astutely sceptical sub-text, Barnardine is centrally important. Contrary to Wilson Knight's claim that the title of the play cites St Matthew's injunction of caution (7:1–2, 'Judge not, that ye be not judged . . .'),[5] the Duke indicates that it means 'Eye for eye, tooth for tooth':

> 'An Angelo for Claudio, death for death!'
> Haste still pays haste, and leisure answers leisure,
> Like doth quit like, and Measure still for Measure.
>
> (V.1.406–408)

Having invoked this retaliatory ethic, the Duke proceeds to demonstrate a clement ethic. The cogency of Angelo's early

---

[5] Verse 2 says, 'For with what judgment ye judge, ye shall be judged: and with what measure ye mete, it shall be measured to you again.'

defence of practical justice has criticised the sentimentality of undiscriminating clemency; but the stubborn pride of Barnardine's character has criticised the naïvety of undiscriminating severity.

We see more than the Duke does, for we can also see the Duke; and it does no harm if, for a while, we see him through the bleary but defiant eyes of Barnardine.

AFTERTHOUGHTS

1

In the light of Watts's argument on pages 33–34, can you think of any other Shakespeare characters that might be considered 'redundant'?

2

How do *you* respond to the 'blatant use of coincidence' (page 34) in *Measure for Measure*?

3

Explain Watts's contention that 'the confrontation between the Duke and Barnardine is part of that sequence of events in which a critical sub-text seems to be challenging the dominant text' (page 37–38). Do you agree?

4

How would you wish an audience to respond to Barnardine, if you were directing *Measure for Measure* (see page 39)?

Mark Spencer Ellis

*Mark Spencer Ellis is Head of English
at Forest School, and a Chief Examiner
in English A level for the London
Schools Examinations Board.*

ESSAY

Heads and maidenheads

Despite the moderation implicit in its title, *Measure for Measure*
is a play of extremes. Its themes cover a variety of paired
opposites: life and death, chastity and incontinence, justice and
mercy, and sin and forgiveness. In form the play switches from a
realistic, potentially tragic beginning to a theatrically contrived
comic ending with religious overtones. The 'heads and maidenheads' motif which I intend to explore in this essay is one of the
main devices which enable Shakespeare to exert some control
over his range of dramatic material. In the first half of the play,
which centres on Claudio's imminent execution and Isabella's
potential violation, the motif lends itself to serious psychological
drama. In the second half, it is integral to the sequence of
theatrical substitutions whereby the plot is moved towards its
comic resolution.

Measure for Measure begins with an image of a head being
stamped on a coin. 'What figure of us think you he will bear?'
(I.1.16) the Duke asks, shortly before making Angelo his deputy.
And Angelo's response takes up the image of 'coining' implicit in
the Duke's words:

> Now, good my lord,
> Let there be some more test made of my metal

Before so noble and so great a figure
Be stamped upon't.

(I.1.47–50)

The formality of this opening scene, accentuated by the rather abstract language, makes the significance of the Duke's actions unclear. However, in giving Angelo his head — both literally and metaphorically — he has given him absolute power over his subjects. In Vienna, 'Mortality and mercy' (I.1.44), death and life, will be in his sole control.

The effects of the Duke's actions become apparent in the play's second scene, where we are given evidence to suggest that Angelo sees his new role more in terms of 'mortality' than 'mercy'. We are no longer in the abstract corridors of power but in one of the 'dark corners' of Vienna where we are given a swift but vivid impression of the moral laxity of the town. In quick succession we meet the decadent Lucio, his companions, the bawd, Mistress Overdone, and her pimp, Pompey. We sense that sexual licence has been rampant, that sexual disease is rife, and that Angelo has started to clean up the town. We hear that he has issued a proclamation closing down the brothels in the suburbs of Vienna. We also meet the pregnant Juliet and her lover, Claudio and we learn that they have become innocent victims of Angelo's purge. Angelo has chosen to make an example of Claudio, who has been sentenced to death for 'fornication', the first of a chain of 'measures' which will link heads and maidenheads. Lucio is quick to indulge in a laboured joke on the double significance of the word 'head':

... an thy head stands so tickle on thy shoulders that a milkmaid, if she be in love, may sigh it off

(I.2.171–173)

— where 'it' may be taken to refer both to Claudio's head and to the milkmaid's maidenhead. The scene ends with what might be seen as a grimmer 'joke', as Claudio asks Lucio to visit Isabella in the hope that she might persuade Angelo to save his life. Isabella is about to become a novice. In becoming a nun she would be entering a cloister, where her maidenhead would be preserved. In abandoning the cloister, she has to return to the life of Vienna where, in attempting to save her brother's life, her maidenhead will be placed in jeopardy.

In the two scenes where Isabella pleads with Angelo for Claudio's life, her moral frame of reference is shown to be very similar to Angelo's. She begins her pleading by showing that she regards lechery with a fiercely puritan revulsion:

There is a vice that most I do abhor,
And most desire should meet the blow of justice

(II.2.29–30)

These lines might be taken as a serious echo of Lucio's earlier sarcastic response on hearing of Claudio's predicament:

LUCIO   What's thy offence, Claudio?
CLAUDIO   What but to speak of would offend again.
LUCIO   What, is't murder?

(I.2.133–136)

Isabella's words imply that, in her eyes, her brother's 'offence' *is* as reprehensible as 'murder', and in the phrase, 'the blow of justice', she suggests that she, like Angelo, sees the executioner's axe as a proper punishment for the crime. Left to herself, Isabella would have been easily persuaded by Angelo's argument that both the 'vice' and its perpetrator must die. In the event, it is Lucio, the open advocate of lust, who provides the spur to make Isabella plead for mercy not with coldness but with passion. And, ironically, once subjected to her passionate argument, Angelo discovers in himself not mercy, but lust; not an inclination to spare Claudio's head, but a desire to seduce Isabella.

Once Angelo has discovered that he is only 'angel on the outward side', the drama enters a new phase. First Angelo craftily and evasively offers Isabella her brother's life in exchange for her virginity. Then Isabella, without evasion, asks Claudio to choose between his own death and her dishonour. In both scenes the characters make disturbing self-discoveries. In both scenes the stakes are Claudio's head and Isabella's maidenhead.

Angelo's attempted seduction of Isabella is given particular power because at the same time that he is pursuing Isabella, he is giving full vent to expressing his horror at the 'crime' that Claudio has committed — the very 'crime' which Angelo desperately yearns to commit. Once again the link between lechery and murder is explored. In a language made extra-ordinary by its mad logic and by its prurient combination of lust and disgust, Angelo argues that to pardon fornication (coining 'heaven's image/ In stamps that are forbid') would be as wrong as pardoning homicide (stealing 'a man already made'):

> Ha! fie, these filthy vices! It were as good
> To pardon him that hath from nature stol'n
> A man already made as to remit
> Their saucy sweetness that do coin God's image
> In stamps that are forbid . . .
>
> (II.4.42–46)

In these lines Angelo sees himself as judge. But in the amplification of the lines which immediately follow, the emphasis is not on the moral dimensions of judgement, but on the ease with which both murder and fornication can be committed.

> . . .'tis all as easy
> Falsely to take away a life true made
> As to put metal in restrainèd means
> To make a false one.
>
> (II.4.46–49)

These words become prophetic in that, once he believes himself to be guilty of having taken Isabella's maidenhead, Angelo will slip easily into murder by conspiring to have Claudio executed in an attempt to cover his traces.

Having established a link between fornication and murder, Angelo proceeds, with even more tortured logic, to offer Isabella the chance of saving Claudio by committing the very sin for which Claudio has been condemned — the sin which Angelo has just 'proved' to be as culpable as murder:

> Which had you rather, that the most just law
> Now took your brother's life, or to redeem him
> Give up your body to such sweet uncleanness
> As she that he hath stained?
>
> (II.4.52–55)

Isabella is too innocent to grasp the purpose behind Angelo's mad argument. However, as their dialogue develops she begins to reveal something of her own repressed sexuality. When asked what she would do to save her brother, she answers with an image in which death and sexuality are strangely intermingled:

> . . . were I under the terms of death,
> Th'impression of keen whips I'd wear as rubies,
> And strip myself to death as to a bed
> That long I have been sick for, ere I'd yield
> My body up to shame.
>
> (II.4.100–104)

Isabella means to say that, rather than yield her 'body up to shame', she would suffer death preceded by terrible agony. However, her language fails to indicate that the whipping would be painful to her. Instead she implies a martyr's delight in suffering. Her words suggest that she would find ecstasy in her pain, the blood of suffering ('rubies') to be treasured and displayed for all to see. The potentially masochistic significance of whipping is further enforced by the sexual connotations of the language — 'strip', 'bed' and 'keen' (which could mean both 'sharp' and 'sexually eager'). Even more revealing is the way in which the personification of death shifts through her speech from an image of a beadle who is whipping her to the image of a lover and then to the image of the bed for which she longs. What is more, Isabella's 'longing' for death is a 'sick' longing suggesting, not so much the desire of a woman for a man, as the craving of a woman who is pregnant. Momentarily at least, Isabella imagines that in a martyr's death she would find the kind of sexual fulfilment which would be denied to her were she to enter the nunnery.

Angelo, discovering that Isabella's facility in argument is not matched by an ability to follow the sub-text to his own argument, is eventually forced to abandon craft and to proposition her directly:

> Redeem thy brother
> By yielding up thy body to my will,
> Or else he must not only die the death,
> But thy unkindness shall his death draw out
> To lingering sufferance.
>
> (II.4.163–167)

Faced with this choice, Isabella's decision is unambiguous. Her maidenhead is too high a price to pay to save her brother's life:

> Then, Isabel, live chaste, and, brother, die.
> More than our brother is our chastity.

(II.4.184–185)

Isabella's decision is unequivocal, but with the character-istic, somewhat egocentric, honesty of a young idealist, she does not just abandon Claudio to his fate; she turns to him to endorse the moral decision she has taken. When Isabella arrives in Claudio's cell, he has been well prepared for death by the hypnotic rhetoric of the Duke. He has momentarily accepted that death can be regarded as a welcome release from the pain and uncertainty of being. But once Isabella reveals that there is 'a devilish mercy' in the judge, and that the 'remedy' which Angelo has offered to save Claudio's head is the surrender of her maidenhead, both the life force in Claudio and his fear of death begin to revive. His mind rejects the comforting advice offered to him by the Duke, as his imagination begins to explore the concrete reality of death:

> Ay, but to die, and go we know not where,
> To lie in cold obstruction and to rot

(III.1.121–122)

To add to the dramatic complexity of the encounter, the phrase 'to die' has sexual connotations. It was often used by the Elizabethans as a euphemism for the experience of orgasm. In vividly expressing his horror of death, Claudio finds words which come close to expressing something of Isabella's un-expressed horror of the loss of self implicit in the sexual act. The confrontation between brother and sister is given further irony by their very different attitudes towards losing heads and maidenheads. We have heard Isabella talk of death in a language which suggests that it will be a sensual, mystical release — something to be desired, rather than feared; we know that Claudio, before receiving Angelo's sentence, kept company with men-about-town like Lucio, for whom the loss of a maidenhead was a 'game of tick-tack' (I.2.189). In asking his sister to spare him, Claudio can argue that he is requesting her to commit a relatively trivial 'sin' which — in the context — should be regarded as a virtue. We know that Isabella sees the act she would have to commit as a vice, comparable to murder. Claudio's 'Sweet sister, let me live' (III.1.136) unleashes a hysterical outburst from his sister, culminating in her harsh judgement, ''Tis best that thou diest quickly' (III.1.154). With Claudio's unfinished, broken interjection, 'O hear me, Isabella' (III.1.154), it seems as though the conflict between brother and sister must end in the degradation and humiliation of both. However, with the re-entry of the Duke, who has been listening to their encounter, the play undergoes an instant change of gear, the 'heads and maidenheads' motif entering into a new phase.

Whether we regard the Duke as a symbol of divine authority, or as an ineffectual renaissance ruler, or as a mere dramatic device, it is clear that from the moment of his intervention in Act III scene 1, the plot of the play and the destinies of the characters are in his control. Integral to his manipulation of the action is a chain of substitutions involving first maidenheads and then heads.

The Duke begins by initiating the psychologically implausible but dramatically neat 'bed-trick'. He explains to Isabella the fourfold advantages of a plan whereby she will agree to Angelo's demands but Mariana — once betrothed to Angelo — will take her place in Angelo's bed:

> ... and here, by this is your brother saved, your honour untainted, the poor Mariana advantaged, and the corrupt deputy scaled.

> (III.1.253–255)

But the Duke is not prepared for the depths of corruption in his deputy and, on discovering that the bed-trick has not resulted in Claudio's reprieve, he is forced to initiate the slightly less neat 'head-trick'. The Provost is persuaded to agree to the substitution of first Barnardine's and then Ragozine's head for Claudio's.

The Duke's abortive attempt to have Barnardine executed brings into focus the changing fortunes of Pompey, whose progress through the play serves to highlight relationships between two of the 'dark corners' of Vienna, the brothel and the prison. Disregarding the nunnery and 'the moated grange' (one a real, the other a fictional escape from the problems of sexuality), there are three main imaginative settings in *Measure for Measure*. At one extreme, there is the world of Mistress Overdone and her girls and clients. Mistress Overdone trades in lechery. She is the great procurer and distributor of 'maidenheads'. At the other extreme, there is the world of the prison, ruled over by the figure of Abhorson, the executioner, who deals in 'heads'. The complex parallels between brothel and prison are highlighted by the career of Pompey. Pompey begins the play as a bawd. In his own words he is 'a poor fellow that would live' (II.1.212). When asked by Escalus whether or not his is a 'lawful trade', he replies, 'If the law would allow it, sir' (II.1.216). Later, in prison, Pompey becomes Abhorson's assistant. 'Can you cut off a man's head?' (IV.2.1–2) the Provost asks. Pompey quibbles laboriously with the implications of 'man's head' and 'woman's head' (i.e. maidenhead) before accepting. He then muses on the strangeness of a career where he has 'been an unlawful bawd time out of mind' but where he is about to become 'a lawful hangman' (IV.2.15). The name 'Abhorson' can be taken to mean 'son of a whore', but the master hangman is initially reluctant to employ a bawd in his trade, claiming that Pompey will 'discredit' the hangman's 'mystery' — the term 'mystery' implying that hanging is a reputable, skilled trade. Pompey argues that the 'painting' — whereby whores prepare their faces as a bait for their clients — can be regarded as a form of 'mystery'. And the Provost's response — 'Go to, sir, you weigh equally. A feather will turn the scale' (IV.2.27–28) — is clearly intended to show that though one 'trade' is lawful and the other not, both are equally disreputable. Later Pompey remarks on a further similarity between 'Mistress Overdone's own house' (IV.3.2–3) and the world of the prison where he has discovered many of his old customers.

Between these two extreme worlds within Vienna, there is the more conventional, more familiar world from which justice is executed. We return to this world in the play's concluding Act as the Duke (initially disguised as the friar) exposes the full extent of Angelo's hypocrisy. Angelo believes that he is guilty of having seduced Isabella and of having murdered Claudio, though through the Duke's substitutions of Mariana's maidenhead and Ragozine's head he is guilty of neither. Nevertheless, as the scene nears its climax, it seems as though *Measure for Measure* will conclude with an endorsement of the 'an eye for an eye and a tooth for a tooth' philosophy of the Old Testament. The signifi-

cance of the play's title begins to become clear as the Duke turns
to Isabella and asks her to join him in calling for Angelo's head
as a recompense for Claudio's:

> . . . for your brother's life,
> The very mercy of the law cries out
> Most audible, even from his proper tongue,
> 'An Angelo for Claudio, death for death!'
> Haste still pays haste, and leisure answers leisure,
> Like doth quit like, and Measure still for Measure.

> (V.1.403–408)

But, as the scene unfolds, the characters in the play, and the
audience, discover that the Duke is not, as he seems here,
'absolute for death'. He is in the process of carrying out the last
of his moral experiments, testing the true quality of Isabella.
She is about to perform an act of genuine mercy, kneeling with
Mariana to plead for the life of the man whom she still believes
killed her brother. Isabella and Angelo discover that Claudio is
still alive, pardon is the word for all, and the play ends with a
rejection of retributive justice and an affirmation of the doctrine
of forgiveness preached in the New Testament. The title of the
play, we discover, is taken from the well-known passage from
the Gospel according to St Matthew which reads:

> Judge not, that ye be not judged. For with what judgement ye
> judge, ye shall be judged: and with what measure ye mete, it
> shall be measured to you again.

> (Mathew 7:1–2)

How well does the 'heads and maidenheads' motif accord
with this religious interpretation of the ending? Some critics
have argued that *Measure for Measure* is a problem play because
Shakespeare's mind and imagination were divided when he
wrote it. There are a number of historical reasons to explain
why the broad sweep of the plot is dominated by a conventional
and conservative view of the problems of government. We know
that the play was presented at court on 26 December 1604,
shortly after King James I's accession to the throne. We know
that Shakespeare's company had recently become the King's
Men and as such were receiving patronage from James. We
know that the King would have approved of the play's preoccu-

pation with the problems of justice and mercy. We know that Shakespeare gave his Duke Vincentio certain attributes which paralleled character traits of the new king. But we also sense, from almost everything that Shakespeare wrote, that there was an anarchic side to his genius, a distrust of orthodox solutions which invariably led him to dramatise unconventional points of view. So, perhaps the comic and ironic preoccupation with heads and maidenheads was one means by which Shakespeare consciously subverted the play's dominant message — that through the benign political manipulation of a well-meaning autocrat, subjects can be helped to experience the joys of religious forgiveness. There is one last twist in the plot which might be seen to undermine this message. *Measure for Measure* ends with the Duke, having out-played Angelo, making his own bid for Isabella's maidenhead. In fact, he propositions her twice in quick succession. The first occasion follows immediately on his restoring Claudio to her. He blatantly uses the gift of Claudio's 'head' to exert pressure on Isabella to give him her 'hand' in marriage:

> If he be like your brother, for his sake
> Is he pardoned, and for your lovely sake,
> Give me your hand and say you will be mine.

(V.1.487–489)

Then, in the play's concluding lines, the Duke proposes to her a second time:

> Dear Isabel,
> I have a motion much imports your good,
> Whereto if you'll a willing ear incline,
> What's mine is yours, and what is yours is mine.

(V.1.531–534)

This time, the language is less bland. In its context, 'What's mine is yours, and what is yours is mine' is, surely, a sexually suggestive line, the impression of parts entwined being accentuated by the 'incline'/'mine' rhyme. And what dowry can Isabella give the Duke in exchange for his title and office, if not her maidenhead, the 'treasure' (II.4.96) once so desired by Angelo?

AFTERTHOUGHTS

1

What links are suggested in this essay between sexuality and death?

2

Do you agree that the 'bed-trick' is 'psychologically implausible' (page 49)?

3

Explain the importance to the play of 'the complex parallels between brothel and prison' identified by Spencer Ellis on page 50.

4

How flattered ought James I have been, in your view, by any parallels between himself and the Duke (page 52)?

Peter Hollindale

Peter Hollindale is Senior Lecturer in English and Education at the University of York. He is General Editor of the Macmillan Shakespeare, and has published numerous books and articles.

ESSAY

The condition of marriage in *Measure for Measure*

Few of Shakespeare's plays excite so much critical disagreement as *Measure for Measure*. Kenneth Muir has pointed to the range of opinions held, and often passionately held, by critics of different persuasions:

> The interpretation of individual plays often depends on the religious opinions of the critics. *Measure for Measure* has been interpreted as an allegory, the Duke representing God, Lucio Lucifer, and Elbow the arm of the law; or, alternatively, as a satire on the idea that the world was providentially governed. During my editorship of *Shakespeare Survey*, I published a number of articles on the play, with the certainty that after each one I would be deluged with indignant rejoinders by critics, repudiating its damnable errors.[1]

Disagreement traditionally extends to the problem of deciding what kind of play it is, a difficulty which has been both recognised and dodged by the expression 'problem play'. The

---

[1] Kenneth Muir, 'The Betrayal of Shakespeare', in *Shakespeare: Contrasts and Controversies* (1985).

term 'problem' in this case refers accurately to both content and genre. *Measure for Measure* is a 'problem play' in that it treats central human experiences, emotions, ideals and principles in a way which eventually seems positive and reassuring, but does so disconcertingly, disturbingly, sceptically, so that we feel the play's humane assertions to be under criticism and waylaid by doubt. Ethically, we do not quite know where we are, because moral certainty seems everywhere to be accompanied by human inadequacy. If the content of the play seems to cause this kind of 'problem', we face the matching difficulty of deciding what kind of genre it belongs to. The play has a 'happy' ending, so it cannot be a tragedy, but we are unlikely to find its last-Act parade of marital solutions unambiguously 'happy', or want to dispense with the inverted commas round the word, so it cannot be simply a comedy either. Recognising that the play falls somewhere between the two, most recent commentators have settled for calling it 'tragi-comedy'.

There is some support for this term from the Italian Renaissance writer Giraldo Cinthio, whose work formed one of the chief sources for the plot of *Measure for Measure.* Cinthio called his own plays 'tragedies', but with a generous and liberal meaning for the word. He said:

> Of the two sorts of tragedy there is one that ends in sorrow. The other has a happy end, but in bringing the play towards its conclusion does not therefore desert the terrible and the compassionable, for without these there cannot be a good tragedy . . . It is in its nature more pleasing to the spectators because it ends in happiness.

Elsewhere, however, he was clearly uneasy about classing this kind of play as tragedy, and so he suggests the alternative, intermediate term which is now widely accepted for *Measure for Measure*:

> But if it displeases you that it should have the name of Tragedy, to satisfy you it could be called Tragicomedy . . . the outcome of which has conformed to comedy — after troubles it is filled with gladness.

This may seem broadly satisfactory for the outcome of *Measure for Measure*, however doubtful we might be about the 'gladness' which is finally achieved. If there are several dubious marriages, at least there are no executions. If justice has followed some devious and arbitrary courses, at least it is tempered with mercy. If human sexuality has shown itself in troubling forms, including not only destructive licence but also destructive repression, at least the institution of marriage has brought desire and instinct within the constraints of social and religious order. The events of the play have shown the potential of human sexual behaviour, both expressive and repressive, to cause pain and suffering and injury, so that the plot has engaged with matters suitable for tragedy, but it has shown how that destructive potential can be neutralised satisfactorily, and offered in conclusion a version of comic harmony.

Act V of *Measure for Measure* is only a *version* of comic harmony, however. Shakespearean comedy habitually ends with a resolution achieved through multiple marriages. They can be found, for example, at the ends of *Love's Labour's Lost, A Midsummer Night's Dream, As You Like It* and *Twelfth Night*. It is not unusual for the marriage-pattern to be varyingly happy and secure, made up of strangely assorted unions with diverse motives, unequal seriousness, and different chances of success. The marriage of Touchstone and Audrey at the end of *As You Like It* is 'but for two months victualled'. The match is between two people with nothing whatever in common except the coarse exchange of sexual pleasure, and it stands in comic contrast to the romantic fulfilments of Rosalind and Orlando, Celia and Oliver. Likewise the concluding marital placements at the end of *Twelfth Night* include the frivolous matrimonial bargain which unites Sir Toby Belch and Maria, a discordant offstage accompaniment to Viola's hard-won romantic match with Orsino. In the comedies which preceded *Measure for Measure*, the final marriage-patterns are *solutions* to the comic disorder of human affairs. Their curious juxtapositions of differing relationships include certain marriages (and these are the most important ones) which are visible *resolutions* also — ceremonious affirmations of achieved and valued love.

By contrast, what we encounter in *Measure for Measure* is a calculated misuse of the former comic pattern: an arrangement of marriages which seems designed to deprive us of secure fulfilments and to emphasise disharmonies. On the face of it the close of *Measure for Measure* observes the comic symmetry of earlier plays. Everything falls into place, and that place is the marriage-bed. Loose ends all appear to be accounted for. Three marriages have taken, or are going to take place, and there is some prospect of a fourth. There are plenty of marital *solutions* at the end of *Measure for Measure*, but if we look for the *resolutions* which are part at least of the closing design in fulfilled comedy, it seems that Shakespeare has deliberately reduced their dramatic importance or left unanswered questions about their likelihood, placing all the stress instead on those unions which are least likely to satisfy our wish for harmonious order. *Measure for Measure* can therefore be regarded not only as a 'tragi-comedy' but as an 'anti-comedy', a play which uses the devices of comedy against itself in order to generate per-turbing and disorientating dramatic effects. What this enables Shakespeare to do is to bring certain ideals and principles — justice, mercy, law, chastity, love — under close and severe scrutiny by putting them into disturbing dramatic proximity with the basic realities of human instinct and desire. Central to this dramatic procedure, I shall argue, is a patterned presenta-tion of marriage, modelled on the accepted forms of comedy, but intended to dislocate our usual expectations.

If for the moment we leave aside the possible but undecided union between the Duke and Isabella, and concentrate first on the marital arrangements of Claudio, Angelo and Lucio, it soon becomes clear that there is remarkable patterning not only in the closing phase of the play but in the earlier circumstances which lead to it. The most important factor uniting them is that all three are partly married before the events of the play begin. Their circumstances are not legally identical. Angelo, who has repudiated Mariana, has a case which is not, whatever its moral weakness, technically deficient in legal strength. It is entirely in character for him to have carefully attended to the fine print of contracts. Dramatically, however, it is the similarity rather than the difference of their cases which is striking, and the repeated pattern is too neat to be accidental.

J W Lever has concisely summarised the situation concerning the secular legalities of marriage (as opposed to its confirmation by religious sacrament):

> While Mariana may fairly be described as Angelo's fiancée, her legal position is rather to be seen as a state of conditional matrimony. English common law recognized two forms of 'spousals'. *Sponsalia per verba de praesenti*, a declaration by both partners that each took the other at the present time as spouse, was legally binding irrespective of any change of circumstances, and, whether the union was later consecrated or not, amounted to full marriage. *Sponsalia per verba de futuro*, a sworn declaration of intention to marry in the future, was not thus absolutely binding. Failure of certain conditions to materialize, notably failure to furnish the agreed dowry, justified a unilateral breach.[2]

Angelo's repudiated contract with Mariana was of this second, conditional kind. The law specified, however, that if a conditional marriage was sexually consummated, it automatically became an absolute marriage, and this is the trap into which Angelo is lured by the bed-trick. Claudio's relationship with Juliet, on the other hand, is of the first and absolutely binding kind. They are legally married, lacking only the final seal of religious sacrament. This he offers in his own defence:

> Thus stands it with me: upon a true contract
> I got possession of Julietta's bed.
> You know the lady. She is fast my wife
> Save that we do denunciation lack
> Of outward order. This we came not to,
> Only for propagation of a dower
> Remaining in the coffer of her friends . . .

> (I.2.144–150)

Setting Claudio's situation alongside Angelo's, we can see the awkward similarities and differences, and through them we run foul of the deliberate confusion into which Shakespeare has poured questions of sexual probity, law, justice and morality. Claudio has broken a law against fornication which is the harsh

---

[2] J W Lever, Introduction to *Measure for Measure*, new Arden edition (London, 1965), pp. liii-liv.

legal enforcement of a *religious* sanction, yet in terms of the law itself his position is a strong one, since he is legally (if not sacramentally) married. In Claudio's plight, law is working against law: one of humanity's ordering artefacts, religion, is working against another, secular contract, and Claudio is trapped as victim in the middle.

Legally Claudio's position is weaker than Angelo's. Claudio, in bedding Juliet, has broken a strict law; Angelo, in dismissing Mariana, has broken neither a religious sanction nor a secular contract. Morally, however, Claudio's position is stronger: his physical adventure with Juliet may be premature and legally dangerous, but it anticipates and expresses a full intention of faithful married love. Angelo, in complete and safe accordance with the law, has behaved with morally indefensible cruelty. Angelo absolves himself from personal moral responsibility by reference to the letter of impersonal law, and his ruthless sexual blackmail of Isabella is merely an extension of this same habitual procedure. It is central to the play's meaning that the law which condemns Claudio should be administered by someone who exhibits an almost identical pattern of human susceptibilities and weaknesses, but shows them in more vicious ways. Both are trapped by sexual appetites, but Claudio the condemned is patently less dishonourable than Angelo the judge. Both, to make the resemblance dramatically clearer, are concerned with money: the history of Claudio's relationship with Juliet, as of Angelo's with Mariana, is governed by consideration of a dowry. Claudio delayed his marriage to Juliet because he was waiting for a dowry; Angelo rejected Mariana in part because her dowry did not meet his expectations. They are men with a similar (and commonplace) pattern of male human weakness, but different ways of showing it. The eventual plight of both is a matter of sexual contract and the match or mismatch of their individual sexual behaviour to the permissions and restraints of secular and religious law.

Repeatedly, the play reminds us of the gap between behaviour and law, between man as instinctual creature and man as lawmaker or lawgiver, between man in life and man in authority. The weight of accusation against Angelo's record as the Duke's deputy is that, while purporting to close the gap between these various roles and functions, he has actually widened it. The most important of many such references in the play is the Duke's in Act V, as he attacks Angelo while seeming to defend him:

> If he had so offended,
> He would have weighed thy brother by himself,
> And not have cut him off.

(V.1. 110–112)

The similarities of conduct between Claudio and Angelo, therefore, are a matter of powerful human and emotional drama but also of intellectual and legal nicety. Their parallel situations give rise to one of several occasions on which *Measure for Measure* causes human instinct, law and morality to meet at a crossroads and fight each other.

There is also the question of Lucio. If we can show that a play repeatedly concerns itself with the same things, and keeps reintroducing them in different guises, we can safely say that this will guide us to its central themes. Before the marital dispositions of Act V, we have seen that Claudio and Angelo have these things in common: they have each contracted in some form to marry a woman; they have had sexual intercourse with the woman before the marriage is confirmed by religious sacrament; they have therefore been guilty of illegal sexual activity carrying the death penalty, or think they have. Lucio's case is not dissimilar. He too has entered into contract, and had sexual relations before marriage; Mistress Overdone tells us so:

> Mistress Kate Keepdown was with child by him in the Duke's time. He promised her marriage. His child is a year and a quarter old, come Philip and Jacob.

(III.2.190–193)

Of course Mistress Kate is a prostitute, and prostitution by its very nature is a triumph of sexual licence over matrimony: hence Angelo's puritanical campaign against the brothels, and hence Lucio's final quasi-comic horror when he is sentenced to marry Mistress Kate: 'Marrying a punk, my lord, is pressing to death, whipping, and hanging' (V.1.519–520). Lucio's condemnation to wedded bliss is the last grotesque example of the play's obsession with the gap between natural man and institutional man. It provides a last coarse highlighting of the divided experience which we have met in subtler and more challenging forms through the behaviour and the penalties which make Claudio and Angelo akin. Lucio is of the selfsame kindred, also, and the play does not allow us to evade the knowledge of it.

There is therefore an evident pattern of similarity in the earlier actions of Claudio, Angelo and Lucio. Important differences exist between them, and these differences are the means by which the play articulates its ideas. In the theatre, however, we are most forcibly struck by the resemblances, and our attention is firmly drawn to them. Nowhere is this more so than in the judicial marriage-broking of Act V, which is a condensed and powerful episode of repetitions and correspondences.

In the past, as we know too well, Claudio has been sentenced to death for his sexual misdemeanours. For him there has been a particularly stark alternative of fates, between the marriage he has partially but willingly enacted and the execution that the law's severity has substituted for it. He it is who expresses most memorably in symbolic terms the play's reiterated pairing of marriage and death, when he says to Isabella:

> If I must die,
> I will encounter darkness as a bride,
> And hug it in mine arms.

(III.1.86–88)

In Act V, Claudio belatedly makes his entry to the Duke's set-piece of mandatory justice still technically a condemned man. Although his pardon is by this stage a foregone conclusion, it must still be formally pronounced by the Duke. So it is, along with the final instruction (needless enough in Claudio's case, but needful for the patterned symmetry of the scene) that he should now complete the rites of marriage and make Juliet an honest woman: 'She, Claudio, that you wronged, look you restore.'

Angelo too is sentenced to death, his perfidy at last exposed. First, however, he is sentenced to marriage. The niceties of marriage-contract, described above, have been ambiguous enough for Mariana to affirm her promise-rights but for Angelo to disclaim his obligations. Once Angelo's guilt is laid open, however, the word 'contract' is a means for simplified enforcement of

Mariana's claims:

> DUKE   ... wast thou e'er contracted to this woman?
> ANGELO   I was, my lord.
> DUKE   Go, take her hence, and marry her instantly.

(V.1.372–374)

Sentence of marriage is to be for Angelo merely the necessary preliminary to sentence of death, which duly follows. Of course, because the play is 'anti-comedy', using comic patterns for its darker purposes, we know already that some well-timed revelations will nullify the death sentence, but we also know that certain characters — notably Mariana and Isabella — are ignorant of what is planned. Pleasure in the skilful play of comic device is mingled for the audience with discomfiture, because real and deep emotions are involved, and because the sacred ritual of marriage and the sombre ritual of execution are being subordinated to the devious convenience of ducal plotting. So, its 'comedy' edged with something more disturbing, the pattern is duly followed through, as Angelo is in turn sentenced to marry, sentenced to die, and pardoned.

In the closing exchanges of the play, Lucio encounters a cruder but equivalent fate, in the main as punishment for presumptuous slander rather than for carnal sin. He too is sentenced to marry (and a prostitute at that); he too is sentenced to die once the marriage is performed; he too is pardoned. 'Comic' as this might be, for Lucio the confirmed penalty of marriage is worse than the remitted penalty of death, or so he says; and however large the pinch of salt with which we take this protestation, it still casts shadows backward on to Angelo and Mariana, and what their inequality of love might mean.

The pattern, at any rate, is clear. All three are pardoned by the Duke. All three are married as an alternative to death, and under judicial compulsion. Marriage, in the sacramental and judicial processes of the Duke's Vienna, seems to be some uncertain halfway house between blessing and punishment.

Whatever the differences, the coincidence of fates is too conspicuous to be overlooked. And for confirmation of the play's device of anti-comedy, we need look no further than the dramatic role of Claudio and Juliet. They are, if anyone is, the Rosalind and Orlando, the Viola and Orsino, of this scene. Theirs is the only prepared and willing sacrament of mutual love. Yet they make a belated entry — dramatic indeed, but chiefly owing to its implications for others rather than themselves — and neither speaks. Of four prospective unions in this scene, the lowest place is accorded to the one which comes closest to romance.

There is no denying that in the finale of *Measure for Measure* a history of sexual transgressions is formally corrected and made acceptable by marriage. Depending on how we interpret the closing state of affairs between the Duke and Isabella, it may be that an unnatural habit of sexual abstention is also corrected by marriage. Marriage, in fact, is a socio-religious device. That sexual activity itself is 'natural' the play has constantly reminded us. Lucio is characteristically the chief spokesman for this viewpoint; he sees it as akin to other animal needs of humankind: 'the vice is of a great kindred. It is well allied, but it is impossible to extirp it quite, friar, till eating and drinking be put down' (III.2.). And he points to sex as a happily convenient social necessity: without it, Vienna will be left unpeopled. However much these may be plausible excuses for mere vice, there is a straightforward biological common sense about them which we cannot ignore. Lucio may be ignobly right, but he is right nevertheless. A similar judgement, if less crudely expressed, comes from no less a person than Escalus, who terms Claudio's misdemeanour a 'fault' (as opposed to sin), whilst the Provost, a figure of intelligence and integrity, describes Claudio as:

> . . . a young man
> More fit to do another such offence
> Than die for this.

(II.3.13–15)

At one level *Measure for Measure* is therefore a morally generous and inclusive play, formidably liberal in the spread of its acceptances. It accepts the practical reality and the necessity and the intense pleasure of human instinct and physical desire; it recognises also the unpleasant truths of carnal selfishness, brutality and exploitation that physical desire can cause; and it accepts the consequent need for social and political constraints to protect the state and keep anarchic physicality in check. Because of its very inclusiveness, *Measure for Measure* permits

its moral design to fall out differently for different readers, audiences, actors and directors, and so invites the passionate disagreements pointed to by Kenneth Muir above.

We can say with certainty that there is a deft symmetrical pattern of situational resemblances in the play which makes these themes unmistakable. I think we can also say with certainty that the play advances a pragmatic and empirical view of marriage. Marriage is a highly efficient socio-political device for the enforcement of physical permissions and constraints. That is how the Duke sees it, and how he uses it.

Beyond this area of certainty, the play is open to many interpretations. It may appear, for example, that sexual licence in Vienna supplies the Duke with a pretext for re-imposing a broader political authority. This is the view considered by Jonathan Dollimore, in an extremely interesting discussion of the play:

> What Foucault has said of sexuality in the nineteenth and twentieth centuries seems appropriate also to sexuality as a sub-category of sin in earlier periods: it *appears* to be that which power is afraid of but in actuality is that which power works through. Sin, especially when internalised as guilt, has produced the subjects of authority as surely as any ideology.[3]

This persuasive viewpoint is a world away from the saintly, providential Duke of other interpretations.

In this essay I have sought to demonstrate some aspects of the play which, whilst they are often ignored, or made subservient to doctrinaire interpretations, seem to me important and beyond dispute. They are, however, only a beginning. This is a play which will always furnish prolific matter for argument, because of its inclusiveness, its even-handedness, and its silences. Among the last are literal silences. We have noted that in the last scene neither Claudio nor Juliet speaks. Nor, at the end, does Isabella. The Duke has twice in public effectively proposed to her, and she says not one word in reply. Much of the

---

[3] Jonathan Dollimore, 'Transgression and Surveillance in *Measure for Measure*', in Jonathan Dollimore and Alan Sinfield (eds), *Political Shakespeare* (Manchester, 1985), p. 85.

play's meaning and effect will depend, in any production, on how the director and the actress use that silence. In this most generous of plays, Shakespeare has left the final word with them, and with us.

AFTERTHOUGHTS

1

What distinction does Hollindale draw between *'solutions'* and *'resolutions'* (page 57)?

2

Why does Hollindale suggest that *Measure for Measure* could be described as an 'anti-comedy' (page 57)? Do you agree?

3

What do *you* feel the 'inequality of love' between Angelo and Mariana 'might mean' (page 62)?

4

What do you understand by 'a pragmatic and empirical view of marriage' (page 64)?

Graham Holderness

Graham Holderness is Head of the Drama Department at Roehampton Institute, and has published numerous works of criticism.

ESSAY

Crossing the moat: Mariana

Mariana is hardly a central character in *Measure for Measure*. She is quite unheard of in the play until introduced into conversation by the Duke in Act III scene 1. She then appears for the first time in Act IV scene 1; pops up again in a brief (15-line) linking scene, IV.6; and is brought in, initially veiled, to help accomplish the Duke's object lesson in poetic justice in the final scene, V.1.

Her function in the play is quite literally that of a convenience to the plot. How is the Duke to save Claudio's life, preserve Isabella's chastity, and yet permit Angelo to pursue his course of irresponsible licentiousness to the extreme limit? Enter Mariana, formerly espoused to and abandoned by Angelo. Under cover of the darkness calculated by Angelo to conceal his clandestine vice, substitute the previous object of legal attachment for the present object of criminal lust. Angelo sins, Claudio lives, Isabella continues a virgin; and Mariana tricks her former fiancé into the physical union which under Elizabethan law converted 'engagement' ('affiance') to full common-law marriage.

Thus Mariana can be seen as one of the play's victors: she succeeds in forcing the man who deserted her to honour his promise of marriage; she acquires the husband she formerly wanted; she redeems herself from a life of melancholy isolation. But she achieves all this by continually offering herself to others as an object of manipulation. She serves the Duke's turn, accepting a role in his Machiavellian plot. She agrees to impersonate Isabella, making love to a man who believes she is someone else. The husband she wins for herself is a penitent and contrite sinner, humiliated and chastised by the public disclosure of his private corruption.

Yet for some reason the figure of Mariana both fascinates and perturbs the imagination, refusing any easy reduction to the mere functionality of a conventional device of plot. In the early nineteenth century Tennyson wrote two poems about her, 'Mariana' (1830) and 'Mariana in the South' (1833). Both poems attempt to describe the emotional condition of restless melancholy endured by Mariana in the 'moated grange' of her isolation. In each, physical descriptions of house and countryside construct a psychological landscape of weary neglect, nostalgic sadness, haunted despondency. The later poem, written after Tennyson had travelled in Europe, is set in the dry and blistering sterility of a southern landscape. The earlier and more successful poem transplants Mariana to England, drawing its vision from the 'dark fen' and the 'glooming flats' of the east coast, the characteristic contours of Tennyson's own Lincolnshire:

> With blackest moss the flower-plots
> > Were thickly crusted, one and all:
> The rusted nails fell from the knots
> > That held the pear to the gable-wall.
> The broken sheds looked sad and strange:
> > Unlifted was the clinking latch;
> Weeded and worn the ancient thatch
> > Upon the lonely moated grange.
> She only said, 'My life is dreary,
> > He cometh not', she said;
> She said, 'I am aweary, aweary,
> > I would that I were dead!'

Out of the dramatic complexity of the play, Tennyson teases a statement of lyric intensity: a single state of emotional being, expressed through a static narrative of unchanging conditions, and through graphic and detailed physical descriptions of exterior objects. In both his poems, the object of focus is that single condition of existence: there is no ultimate release for

Mariana, as there is in Shakespeare's play, from the imprisonment of loneliness.

One way of evaluating this 'imaginary biography' of Mariana
would be to relate it to those currents of curiosity (satirised by
L C Knights in his famous essay 'How Many Children had Lady
Macbeth?') which sought to fabricate an imaginary 'life' for a
dramatic character by speculating possibilities outside the
action of the play. Did Lady Macbeth have any children, and if
so what happened to them? What did Hamlet study at university
in Wittenberg? How had Cordelia been treated by her sisters
before the opening scene of *King Lear*? A particular focus of this
curiosity in the nineteenth century were the extra-dramatic
lives of the women in Shakespeare's plays, thoroughly investi-
gated in *The Girlhood of Shakespeare's Heroines*. Modern literary
criticism would tend to regard Tennyson's poem as a kind of
imaginative playfulness, having little to do with a serious critical
interest in the play.

Tennyson's depiction of Mariana can also be related to
particular Victorian methods of representing women. Like
Dante Gabriel Rossetti's 'The Blessed Damosel', or Tennyson's
own more famous 'The Lady of Shalott', the fairy-tale image of
the beautiful woman shut away in a tower, living a life of
dream-like intensity cut off from ordinary social intercourse,
was a common focus of Victorian poetic fantasies. But 'Mariana'
is much more than that. Where 'The Lady of Shalott', with its
setting in medieval legend, invokes romantic and chivalric ideas
about women, 'Mariana' is both more modern and more general
in its focus. The poem depicts not only the isolation of the
woman in Shakespeare's play, but a condition of existential
isolation, applicable in some ways to every human being. In this
respect Tennyson's poem relates closely to a poem by Matthew
Arnold ('To Marguerite', 1853):

> Yes: in the sea of life enisl'd
> With echoing straits between us thrown,
> Dotting the shoreless watery wild,
> We mortal millions live alone.

The image that Tennyson derived from Shakespeare, of the
individual isolated in a house surrounded by a moat, becomes in
Arnold's poem an image of the modern condition, in which each

human being is an island separated from every other by a gulf of impassable separation, the 'unplumbed, salt, estranging sea'. John Fowles in his novel *The French Lieutenant's Woman* (1977) quotes Arnold's poem as an example of the Victorian fore-shadowing of modern existentialism. We could suggest, then, that Tennyson's imagination was drawn towards Shakespeare's Mariana for more substantial reasons than a playful curiosity about the hidden biography which could be imagined beyond the world of the play (where of course we see Mariana only in the company of other people).

Mariana fascinates, compels the imagination. She also disturbs, introduces into the reader's or spectator's response a quality of intractable difficulty. In a 'problem' play, Mariana is one of the chief problems. The editor of the Arden edition of *Measure for Measure*, texts which generally operate to produce for Shakespeare's plays the most traditional and normative interpretations, spends four pages of his introduction worrying about Mariana, and about the play's reliance on the device of the 'bed-trick' or 'substituted bedmate' for the achievement of its precarious moral balance. In this conventional reading, the Duke is seen consistently as an unexceptionable character, a type of the ideal ruler whose every action and sentiment can be justified as legal, moral and providentially just. But the 'problematical' quality of this aspect of the play lies in the distinct possibility of other, less sympathetic readings.

It is of course morally possible (which is not the same thing as dramatically probable, given the non-realistic convention of the 'disguised ruler' with which the play operates) for the Duke to reveal himself at any moment to stop Angelo's misconduct. Instead he operates as an *agent provocateur*, advising Isabella to make the assignation with Angelo, and persuading Mariana to keep it. In Act IV scene 1 where the Duke brings Isabella and Mariana together, there is a certain coy slyness in the way the two women 'walk aside' to discuss the details of the 'bed-trick'. When they return the Duke goes to some trouble to assure Mariana of the morally unexceptionable character of what she has undertaken to do:

> Nor, gentle daughter, fear you not at all.
> He is your husband on a pre-contract.

> To bring you thus together, 'tis no sin,
> Sith that the justice of your title to him
> Doth flourish the deceit.

(IV.1.70–74)

The Arden editor takes this assurance as a complete justification of the Duke's actions. Admitting that the preservation of one woman's chastity by sacrificing another's might 'offend present-day susceptibilities', the editor insists that 'Shakespeare's handling of the device shows a careful provision to meet such objections' (p. liii). The Duke's position is then justified by reference to the Elizabethan laws of marriage, which contained a provision for a kind of 'conditional matrimony', a sworn declaration to marry at some time in the future. This is the 'pre-contract' that Angelo swore with Mariana. In the guise of a friar, the Duke then can be seen as an authority on such questions of matrimonial law. On the other hand, the Arden editor goes on, churchmen regarded sexual union on the basis of the 'pre-contract' espousal as sinful. But of course the Duke isn't a friar but a monarch: so he is upholding the validity of secular law. Besides, the Duke in the play is really a symbol for James I, who was titular head of the Church: so his handling of the matter, however equivocal, would have been acceptable to a contemporary audience as validated by both religious and secular authority, an unquestionable 'final ruling' (p. lv).

This Jesuitical sophistication is worthy of the Duke himself; and if anything the modern critic's arguments are even more equivocal than the fictional Duke's moral protests. Within the context of the play, where the relationship of Angelo and Mariana is only one of three similar couplings, there is much more pressure on the reader to conclude that the Duke 'doth protest too much' for his explanations to be wholly convincing. The obvious comparison is with the union of Claudio and Juliet, where sexual congress has taken place on the basis of a 'pre-contract' without full sanctity of marriage. Angelo's attempt to punish this union is of course seen as an enormous injustice, a perspective which in turn validates the romantic irresponsibility of the young couple who couldn't wait. The Duke's manipulation of Angelo and Mariana can be seen as an inversion of Angelo's abuse of the law: where initially the law is used to punish and separate the victims of natural passion, the Duke uses justice to re-unite by passion the betrayer and his abandoned fiancée.

But the comparison does not stand up very well to closer scrutiny. Claudio and Juliet chose one another as partners, swore their pre-contract, made love before proper marriage, and have no desire other than to stay together and become fully man and wife. The law in this context is a kind of technicality which interferes with a natural and admirable fidelity. In the case of Angelo and Mariana, the law is used, together with the bed-trick, as a form of duress, a means of forcing Angelo to honour his provisional marriage. The passion involved is also very different from the impatient desires of Claudio and Juliet, being a vicious and exploitative lust for Isabella.

The elaborate procedures of manipulation and disclosure used to incriminate and convict Angelo, operating as they do through deceit and dark conspiracy, seem to make the Duke and Angelo counterparts rather than opposites. And although in the play's final scene the Duke seems intent on provoking in Angelo as much guilt and self-recrimination as possible, it is hard to avoid the implication that marriage to Mariana is inflicted on him as a form of punishment. The presence in the play of the bawd Pompey, and the ambiguous figure of Lucio, tends to draw these potential implications further out. Pompey's occupation, which is of course that of a 'pimp' procuring customers for prostitutes, seems to offer an uneasy angle of perspective on the Duke's bringing together of Angelo and Mariana. At the play's opening, Lucio correctly identifies the passion of Claudio and Juliet as natural rather than vicious, and thus puts himself clearly on the side of the play's morality. His sardonic references to the supposedly absent Duke (who is of course, unfortunately for him, very much present) as a notorious libertine, seem to the reader appropriately comic exaggerations of the Duke's actual chicanery and manipulation. But the Duke himself is very hard on Lucio, and punishes him with enforced marriage to the prostitute he has made pregnant. The reader/spectator is thus offered a comparative choice. Which coupling more closely resembles the judicial enforcement of marriage between Angelo and Mariana: the romantic attachment of Claudio and Juliet, which is based on mutuality and free choice; or the sinful intercourse of Lucio with the prostitute he is obliged, by the authority of the ruler, to take as his wife?

Mariana then fascinates the imagination, and contributes significantly to the play's 'problematical' quality, its apparent ambiguity on the very moral questions it seems designed to explore. As this equivocal figure, she makes clear and definite interpretation difficult. It is obviously possible, as the Arden editor attempts, to re-write in interpretation this aspect of the play, so as to produce an impeccably correct moral balance. But the critical arguments then seem unconvincing, since they so evidently rely on the oversimplification of complexities and the smoothing of unevenness.

As a female figure, Mariana can offer to modern interpretation the option of another reading, of the kind preferred by feminist theory. Mariana's 'problem' would be related in this context to the oppressed and unequal position of women in the society depicted. Initially under the protection of her brother, about to be handed over to another man in marriage, Mariana is robbed by her brother's death of both her masculine supports. Her doom of isolation could then be seen as the natural condition of women in such a society; and her determination to win back her rights could further be viewed as an admirable example of female enterprise and independence, a positive role-model for women. In this context Mariana appears at the play's conclusion to be a victor, her chastened husband committed to her authority and control rather than the other way round.

This argument also presents difficulties. Mariana seems on the evidence of the play to be dramatically interesting only in the space between her assignment to figures of masculine power, brother or husband. Both her brother's death and married life with Angelo lie outside the compass of the drama. Whatever Mariana becomes in our acts of interpretation must depend on what is given by the play. There is the woman alone and abandoned in the moated grange, Tennyson's Mariana, whose condition provokes compassion. And there is the woman prepared to trick her former suitor into bed to force a marriage, whose actions provoke a disturbed sense of moral ambiguity, a contradictory mixture of sympathy and repugnance, of admiration and (certainly in the male reader/spectator) fear.

AFTERTHOUGHTS

1

What do you understand by *'agent provocateur'* (page 70)?

2

What do you understand by 'Jesuitical sophistication' (page 71)?

3

Do you agree that Angelo and the Duke can be seen as 'counterparts rather than opposites' (page 72)?

4

To what extent do you feel a 'mixture of sympathy and repugnance' for Mariana (page 73)?

Rachel Redford

Rachel Redford is an Adult Education teacher in Bristol, Moderator for GCSE English for the Southern Examining Group, and Assistant Chief Examiner for A-level English for the University of London Schools Examinations Board.

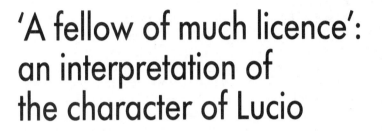

ESSAY

'A fellow of much licence': an interpretation of the character of Lucio

Measure for Measure is a play about ambiguity and ambivalence. It poses deep questions about the law, judgement and mercy, and stimulates the mind by giving no absolute answers. In this play of ideas where characters are not what they appear to be, we are never quite sure what 'our seemers be' (I.3.54): the vibrant 'fantastic', Lucio, is perhaps the most intriguing character of them all. Lucio appears in only six of the play's fifteen scenes and, apart from one speech in I.4, he speaks at most six lines at a time, more usually merely a few words. He is a shaft of light flickering through the play, and the brevity of his lines contributes to his energy which makes him 'a kind of burr' (IV.3.175) that sticks in the audience's vision and mind.

That Lucio's name recalls Lucifer, the light-bearing archangel who rebelled against God, is no accident. Lucio is a rebel. He seems to shift his ground at different points in the play, and yet there is a consistent truth about him. He sees the light and, frequently swearing 'by my troth', seems to know truths which other characters do not. He is shrewd; his vision is clear-sighted. Significantly, Shakespeare gives Lucio the lines which express what is perhaps the moral of the play, *'Cucullus non facit monachum'* (V.1.261) (the hood does not make the monk): appearances are not what they seem.

Lucio is first seen in the play at ease with the two Gentlemen. With their good-natured banter thick with puns relating to prostitution and venereal disease, Lucio appears relaxed and quick witted. The Second Gentleman has come to 'three thousand dolours a year' (I.2.49) through his infections caught under Mistress Overdone's roof. 'Ay, and more,' adds the First Gentleman, and Lucio's following quip, 'A French crown more' (I.2.51), shows both the facility of his verbal punning and his worldly realism which enables him to regard with humour the miseries of the 'French disease', and the symptomatic bald head of its sufferer. As is the case throughout *Measure for Measure*, Lucio is not merely providing comic relief, although these exchanges do produce necessary laughter in this serious play. With his mention of the 'sanctimonious pirate' (I.2.7) who scratched out 'Thou shalt not steal' from his Ten Commandments, Lucio is seen from the outset as being aware of the difference between public morality and private behaviour is — the question at the heart of *Measure for Measure*. With Mistress Overdone's sudden news of Claudio's imminent death, Lucio shows his first quicksilver change and switches immediately into brusque, dynamic common sense: 'Away. Let's go learn the truth of it' (I.2.80). Lucio's words are characteristically vigorous, practical and direct, and show him as a man who searches for the truth, the Light of his name. He sees immediately the absurdity of a 'neglected act' (I.2.169) which condemns a man to death for a mere 'game of tick-tack' (I.2.189), and is swift to offer sensible help to Claudio.

In addressing Isabella with infinite respect and grace, Lucio shows another facet:

> I hold you as a thing enskied and sainted,
> By your renouncement an immortal spirit
> And to be talked with in sincerity,
> As with a saint.

(I.4.34–37)

This is the Lucio who has previously been seen at familiar ease with lechery and who usually seems with women, as he says, 'the lapwing . . . to jest,/ Tongue far from heart' (I.4.32–33). The consequence of what he called Claudio's 'rebellion of a cod-piece' (III.2.109) and 'untrussing' (III.2.169) is here described in delicate fruitful terms:

> . . . even so her plenteous womb
> Expresseth his full tilt and husbandry.
>
> (I.4.43–44)

It is the consummate ease with which Lucio moves from one role to another which contributes to his ambiguity. Is he genuinely horrified at Claudio's plight and truly awed by Isabella's purity — or is he a soldier thwarted 'in hand and hope of action' (I.4.52) waiting for a chance to attack Authority and using all his urbane charm to manipulate this pawn in his attack?

This same ability to manipulate is seen by Lucio's asides throughout Act II scene 2, when he stage-manages Isabella's pleading with Angelo. Lucio's asides in this scene are sometimes seen as merely comic — 'You are too cold' (line 56), 'O, to him, to him, wench, (line 124) — and undoubtedly there is in his comments a comic theatricality reducing the high solemnity of the scene. But they also reveal a clear-sighted Lucio who knows exactly what he is doing. Isabella's words:

> O, 'tis excellent
> To have a giant's strength, but it is tyrannous
> To use it like a giant.
>
> (lines 107–109)

elicit Lucio's significantly vigorous endorsement: 'That's well said' (line 109). Lucio is in rebellion against harshly judgemental Authority, and Isabella can be seen here as his agent.

Lucio shows this same apparent two-sidedness in his treatment of Pompey, the 'wicked bawd', his associate and supposed friend. Having shown such concern for Claudio, he harshly dismisses Pompey who has been condemned by the same senseless law:

> Well, then, imprison him. If imprisonment be the due of a bawd, why, 'tis his right.
>
> (III.2.63)

He is deaf to Pompey's pleading for Lucio to stand him bail:

> No, indeed will I not, Pompey; it is not the wear. I will pray,
> Pompey, to increase your bondage.

> (III.2.70).

Measure for Measure constantly encourages us to question, and
Lucio's treatment of Pompey is so exaggerated, so theatrical:

> Go to kennel, Pompey, go

> (III.2.81)

that we question his motives. Could it be that this is not Lucio
simply displaying duplicity but, on the contrary, being single-
mindedly consistent? Does he know full well that the friar in
front of whom he makes this display is really the Duke, and this
show of support for the law is for his benefit? In this play of
constant role-playing, it seems a plausible interpretation.

All the other characters accept unquestioningly the Duke's
departure; only Lucio has the insight not to do so. In the only
extended speech he makes in the whole play, in I.4, he refers to
the Duke having 'strangely gone from hence' (line 50) and states
clearly:

> His givings-out were of an infinite distance
> From his true-meant design.

> (I.4.54–55)

Lucio suspects that the Duke is not dealing plainly, and just as
shrewdly he assesses Angelo as:

> . . . a man whose blood
> Is very snow-broth, one who never feels
> The wanton stings and motions of the sense,
> But doth rebate and blunt his natural edge
> With profits of the mind, study, and fast.

> (I.4.57–61)

With his insight into the human character, Lucio rightly divines
that such a man as Angelo will be easy prey to 'maidens . . .
when they weep and kneel' (I.4.80) as he instructs Isabella to do.
Lucio and the Duke can be seen as master manipulators.

Lucio is shown at his boldest when he speaks with the
disguised Duke. We have already seen that Lucio suspects the

Duke of having 'strangely' gone away. Why should he question this friar who has no apparent connection with the Duke about the Duke's whereabouts unless he suspects his disguise?

> What news, friar, of the Duke?
>
> (III.2.82)

It is generally assumed that Lucio does not realise that he is talking to the Duke and is unwittingly making ultimate trouble for himself by his malicious mischief. Surely Lucio is cleverer than that? As soon as they are alone, Lucio is direct: 'It was a mad fantastical trick of him to steal from the state, and usurp the beggary he was never born to' (III.2.88–89). Is not the Duke disguised as a mendicant friar clearly usurping beggary? As Escalus says, Lucio is a 'fellow of much licence' (III.2.195) and as a fantastic, rather like Lear's 'all-licensed' Fool in *King Lear*, he enjoys a freedom of speech denied to other characters. Far from being malicious gossip, Lucio's words are full of the common sense of a clear-sighted realist, a quality singularly lacking in those in power. Lechery cannot be legislated against, Lucio claims: 'It is well allied, but it is impossible to extirp it quite, friar, till eating and drinking be put down' (III.2.97–98).

Speaking in hard-hitting prose, Lucio shows the same laser accuracy as he caricatures the 'ruthless' Angelo as a 'motion generative', the sexless puppet whose 'urine is congealed ice' (lines 105, 104). When he appears to slander the Duke — 'He had some feeling for the sport. He knew the service, and that instructed him to mercy' (lines 113–114) — is it really slander? We know nothing of the Duke's past, but given the sexual mores of Vienna, it seems quite likely that the Duke is no 'motion generative'. Lucio's sensible point is that the fact that the Duke has been drunk, 'would eat mutton on Fridays' and has been 'your beggar of fifty and his use was to put a ducat in her clack-dish' (lines 119–120) makes him better able to govern with *mercy*, the quality missing from that 'ungenitured agent', Angelo. And surely it is not coincidental that Lucio's sexual innuendo involves a beggar in its metaphor?

The Duke shows the hypocrisy of the ruling class in *Measure for Measure* as he retaliates with authoritative threats and anger. Lucio is insistent, but ignored: 'Sir I know him, and I love him' (line 141); 'Come, sir, I know what I know' (line 144). Whilst

Lucio is licensed by the Duke's disguise, the Duke is constrained by it, left to nurse his hurt pride, the 'back-wounding calumny', and muse on another truth about the impotence of the law when faced with the complexity of human nature, 'What king so strong/ Can tie the gall up in the slanderous tongue' (lines 177–178). To Escalus, the Duke is 'a gentleman of all temperance' (line 227). Lucio is often taken to be a lying scoundrel, but, as always, *Measure for Measure* invites us to look below the surface. As he says, Lucio knows what he knows and is it not entirely plausible that with his easy intimacy with both the high and low life, Lucio does indeed know the truth; whilst Escalus, the revered man of government, sees the Duke's public face only? One of the play's enduring qualities is that it still speaks to us directly and we can immediately think of contemporary analogies.

Lucio clearly has a good opinion of the Duke as a ruler. He comforts Isabella after Claudio's supposed death: 'If the old fantastical Duke of dark corners had been at home, he had lived' (IV.3.155–156). This is no criticism. Lucio accepts the Duke for what he is. He may be a man of intrigue who will go off and do strange things — as did James I in Shakespeare's own time — but at least he would not condemn a man to death for 'untrussing'. Likewise, Lucio's remark 'He's a better woodman than thou tak'st him for' (IV.3.160), which gives the Duke such offence, expresses the quality which makes the Duke a better ruler not a worse one in Lucio's estimation. As Mariana says in the final scene, 'best men are moulded out of faults' (V.1.437). It is ironic that the Duke's 'Well, you'll answer this one day. Fare ye well' (IV.3.161), spoken in anger after Lucio's reference to the Duke's liking for women, comes just after we have seen the Duke cruelly lie to Isabella about her brother's death. The lie, the Duke claims, is:

> To make her heavenly comforts of despair
> When it is least expected.

(IV.3.107–108)

What exquisite hypocrisy! The Duke wants Isabella for himself and believes this despicable piece of deception will further his cause. It is one of the delights of *Measure for Measure* that an opposite case can be made — that the Duke is a force working for a peaceful resolution and the ultimate good of all the characters. It is Lucio's role which reinforces the Duke's ambiguity.

The fact that Lucio admits having lied under oath to the Duke about the paternity of his child is often taken as 'evidence' that Lucio does not know that he is talking to the Duke. The free admission is seen as the foolish scoundrel unwittingly trapping himself by his loose tongue into final marriage with 'the wench' Kate Keepdown. Could it not be seen just as easily as Lucio goading the disguised Duke into revealing his identity, taking further liberties, safe in the knowledge that the Duke is trapped in his disguise? The one truth that *Measure for Measure* presents is that there *is* no one answer, but Lucio's final remark seems to suggest that he has a serious intention: 'I am a kind of burr, I shall stick' (IV.3.175). The Duke would rather this uncomfortable realist disappeared, but Lucio is tenacious. He is a stimulating dramatic device which ensures that the audience constantly questions the surface reality.

A scoundrel of sorts Lucio certainly is, but unlike Angelo and the Duke he does not pretend to be otherwise. He has not upheld his promise to marry Kate Keepdown, and has left her to bear her child alone. When arrested, Mistress Overdone claims that Lucio has informed on her. Out of true charity, another quality lacking in those who rule according to the law, Mistress Overdone has looked after Lucio's child for more than a year. Is this informing on such a woman malicious duplicity on Lucio's part, or is it his way of showing up the absurdity of the law? With Pompey, Mistress Overdone and their kind in prison, will the society of Vienna not have to face the fact that the law is an ass? After all, as Pompey wisely observes, unless the law means to 'geld and splay all the youth of the city' (II.1.219–220), the real problems will not be solved — if indeed they are solvable at all.

The role of Lucio in the long final scene of the play is usually regarded as a comic one, married off to Kate Keepdown as his natural desert, part of the neat tying up of ends in this final scene of resolution. Closer consideration of his part will show that it is not so simple as that. Isabella pleads to the Duke, who is now undisguised but playing the role of the unbelieving figure of authority:

> . . . but let your reason serve
> To make the truth appear where it seems hid,
> And hide the false seems true.

(V.1.65–67)

This surely has been Lucio's aim throughout and it is just after this that he interjects for the first time. These interruptions are undoubtedly comic in their quickness and in the way their cheekiness undermines the legal solemnity of the proceedings:

> DUKE   You were not bid to speak.
> LUCIO   No, my good lord,
>   Nor wished to hold my peace.
> DUKE   I wish you now, then.

(V.1.78–79)

Lucio's undercutting remarks induce laughter in the audience, but, as so often with Lucio, his words seem to have a deeper significance. His cynicism about sexuality in these interjections deepens the audience's laughter: 'Marry, sir, I think, if you handled her privately, she would sooner confess' (lines 274–275); 'That's the way, for women are light at midnight' (line 278). The juxtaposition of Lucio's witty cynicism with Escalus' naïvety further heightens the dramatic effect. The preceding high seriousness of the questioning of the dignified Mariana is immediately deflated by another quip from Lucio:

> LUCIO   My lord, she may be a punk. For many of them are
>   neither maid, widow, nor wife.
> DUKE   Silence that fellow.

(lines 179–181)

The Duke's anger and Lucio's comment makes the procedure suddenly ridiculous and the audience laughs. But Lucio has a serious point. If Mariana is neither spinster, wife nor widow, she might well be a prostitute, but because of her bearing and position in society, the law assumes she is not. Or does he mean that since everyone else in the city seems to be guilty under Angelo's law, why should not Mariana be too? Lucio's apparently comic interjections are thus constantly pointing out the absurdity and hypocrisy of the law.

Even as the Duke is seen to be performing his acts of resolution and forgiveness, Lucio continues to reinforce the Duke's moral ambiguity by maintaining his criticisms of the Duke, now by attributing his own previous apparently outrageous remarks to the elusive friar whom he describes as 'a meddling friar' and a 'saucy friar,/ A very scurvy fellow' (lines 135–136). Just as Escalus's already quoted assessment of the Duke as 'a gentleman of all temperance' (III.2.227) was the opposite to Lucio's, so Lucio's view of the friar opposes that of Friar Peter's: 'I know him for a man divine and holy' (V.1.144). Friar Peter's view can be seen, in Isabella's words, to be that 'the false seems true' (V.1.67), while Lucio's view is one in which the truth appears 'where it seems hid' (V.1.66). The Duke disguised as the friar is, from one point of view, indeed 'meddling', 'saucy' and 'scurvy'. He has abdicated his duty to a man he knows is not worthy of the responsibility, he tells lies and plots to have a compromised novice nun for his own. Lucio's comments force us to remember this side of the Duke.

The climax of Lucio's attack on the Duke comes as Escalus orders the disgraced friar to prison: 'Why you bald-pated, lying rascal, you must be hooded, must you?' (lines 348–349). Lucio has already spoken his wise aphorism *Cucullus non facit monachum* (line 261) which suggests again that he is certain the friar is not who he purports to be. Here he rails, 'Show your sheep-biting face, and be hanged an hour' (lines 350–351). Clearly, Lucio sees the Duke as a wolf in sheep's clothing, a prowler — and in some ways he is right. It is appropriate that Lucio's reaction to revealing the Duke is not spoken, although the Duke's 'Sneak not away, sir' (line 355) suggests that Lucio, his duty done for the moment, is trying to avoid arrest. He does not speak throughout the Duke's meting out of 'justice'. Now that Lucio is silent, no voice expresses surprise or disquiet at the Duke's behaviour.

The Duke gives out forgiveness and justice tempered with mercy to all, pardoning even Barnardine. But to Lucio, he is harsh: 'And yet here's one in place I cannot pardon' (line 496). Angelo has, so he believes, morally blackmailed a novice nun into unlawful sex, abandoned his fiancée, condemned a young man to death for a 'crime' he himself has committed, and broken his word — but the Duke forgives him. Lucio has apparently slandered the Duke and he is condemned to being 'Whipped first' and 'hanged after' (line 504). The severity of the punishment suggests not only that Lucio's slander is probably not slander but the truth; it also points to the absurdity of both the law and the happy-ever-after, redemptive resolution of this last scene.

Lucio's final quip is comic and flippant: 'Marrying a punk, my lord, is pressing to death, whipping, and hanging' (line 519). It neatly ends his contribution with typical disrespect and makes us question the 'justice' of the last scene. What sort of justice metes out marriage as a punishment? What justice is there for poor, abused Isabella, pressurised into yielding her virginity to a man in authority whom she regards as a tyrant, being told by another whom she trusts that her brother is dead when he is not? This morally reprehensible behaviour is implicitly condoned by an offer of marriage from one of her deceivers. It is Lucio's constant, burr-like sticking to the truth, his deliberate undermining of the end's neat resolution, which prevents the audience from feeling that this is a satisfying Romance ending. Isabella is given no opportunity to reply to the Duke. Lucio has undermined our confidence in the ending sufficiently for us to conjecture that perhaps Isabella's answer is a refusal.

AFTERTHOUGHTS

1

Do you agree that Lucio is 'perhaps the most intriguing character of them all' (page 75)?

2

Do you agree that Lucio is 'shrewd' in his assessment of Angelo (page 78)?

3

Does Redford persuade you that Lucio's account of the Duke's sexual history may be accurate (pages 79–80; 84)?

4

Has this essay convinced you that Lucio penetrates the Duke's disguise?

John Saunders

John Saunders is Lecturer in English Literature at the West Sussex Institute of Higher Education, and Awarder in English Literature A level for the Oxford and Cambridge Schools Examinations Board.

ESSAY

What final statement?

So what *does* happen at the end of the play? Isabella can smilingly accept the Duke's offer, indicating the way he has helped her realisation of human qualities. She can passively accept him, suggesting that a woman's sexuality is, ultimately, never hers to control. She can fix him with looks of withering scorn or of total incomprehension to show how astonishing is the implication that she should rearrange her emotions to fall in with the gratefulness the Duke expects as a reward for producing Claudio. Or she can walk off in the opposite direction. Convincing cases can be made for all these endings, although it is unlikely that the last two can have had much theatrical validity before the Twentieth century. However, in spite of the liveliness of debate on this issue, to see Isabella's behaviour in the final moment as crucial to the production is to close down the function of a performance to the limits of a tradition from which Shakespeare's plays broke free.

Ideally, perhaps, it should be left to the person playing the part to do what feels right for each staging. But as things presently stand in the theatre, Isabella's final movement (or lack of movement) can only be seen as a statement by the director of the production. Her acceptance of the Duke points us towards one sort of reading, her denial or reluctance towards another. To see this as a judgement, a summing-up of the issues, is to reduce the play to a lecture, to reduce the part of a director to that of a lecturer, and to make the cast into puppets. There are, of course, plenty of readings of *Measure for Measure* which do exactly that. In their eagerness to confront the issues, they close down the questions raised by the text. They fail to see that it does not really matter what Isabella does. No audience is going to be passive enough to accept such a judgement if it does not match its own responses. The important thing is that the issues should be raised. There is bound to be a significant proportion of those in the theatre who would prefer Isabella to have done something other than what she did. Their disagreement does not invalidate their experience of the performance.

It can be argued that the question of Isabella's response is of very minor importance when considering the major issues raised in the text. If you ask twenty theatregoers (or students of the play) to sum up what happens in no more than fifty words, there are several points which will feature in all the summaries but this particular question is unlikely to be one of them. The aspects of the play which make the greatest impression on us are those which feature most strongly in the source material.[1] The majority of this material concerns the story of The Corrupt Magistrate, the man who offers mercy in some form in exchange for sex. The dramatic pace of the play derives from Angelo's proposal. Both of the other two source elements, The Disguised Ruler and The Substituted Bedmate, are subordinate. Although the Duke's hurried removal from Vienna is the first action of which we are aware, its function is to put the spotlight on Angelo:

> What figure of us think you he will bear?
> For you must know, we have with special soul
> Elected him our absence to supply,
> Lent him our terror, dressed him with our love,
> And given his deputation all the organs
> Of our own power. What think you of it?

> (I.1.16–21)

---

[1] See Geoffrey Bullough, *Narrative and Dramatic Sources of Shakespeare*, vol. 2 (London, 1958), pp. 399–417, or *Measure for Measure*, edited by J W Lever (London, 1965), pp. xxxv–lv.

The first scene provides no hint of the Duke's 'reasons', such as he gives to Friar Thomas (I.3.19–43), and even this explanation of the need to restore order and the rule of law is seen to be secondary in the last part of his speech (lines 43–54) to the testing of Angelo, whose hidden nature is pointed by the final couplet: 'Hence we shall see,/ If power change purpose, what our seemers be.'

It is in our reaction to Angelo's abuse of his authority that the strongest responses to the play are found. It can be held that Isabella's refusal shows up the self-centred nature of her wish to enter a convent, a concern with rules rather than with practical charity. More convincing is the line that her action represents an emancipation of female sexuality, a refusal by woman to be defined by male desire — Angelo's 'Be that you are,/ That is, a woman' (II.4.134–135) amounts to a blunt statement that the essence of womanhood is to be bedded by a man — and that for her to submit is for all women to do so. Less frequently argued is the case for regarding chastity as a positive virtue rather than an absence of experience. Irrespective of the view taken, it is difficult to avoid strong feelings about this crux. While it is possible to engage in a vigorous and clinical debate about whether Cordelia would have done better to join her sisters in flattering her father (*King Lear*, I.1), such a discussion is virtually impossible when examining the question of whether Isabella should give in to Angelo. There is an intensely personal nature about the positions which are taken, and experience of student discussions suggests that there is every chance of strong feeling, acute embarrassment and personal abuse within a few minutes.

I should like to argue that one of the reasons why the ending of the play has posed such difficulties of interpretation is that we tend to carry the strength of our responses to the Angelo/Isabella part of the plot on to the other elements which in structure, but more importantly in the responses they provoke, are essentially comic.

The elements of structure are fairly straightforward, and are certainly not limited to Shakespeare's plays. The first point is that in comedy one has a second chance. Mistakes which in real life cannot be rectified only threaten the characters' future happiness. The happiness which is finally achieved comes about through transparent manipulation of the plot, and there is usually a symmetrical bringing together of several couples in which consideration of whether they are individually suited is outweighed by the general impression of harmony. Such sheer artificiality of structure makes us realise that the problems raised in the plot can only be 'solved' in the world of comedy. Although describing Angelo's behaviour (or that of Juliet and Claudio) as a 'mistake' may not be entirely appropriate, this basic pattern does apply to *Measure for Measure*. Difficulties occur for the audience when we find ourselves watching what we recognise as comic but retaining the strength of feeling from an episode which demands a deeply personal commitment to one view or another. Isabella is where these responses collide; she is the play's battleground. She is centrally involved in the comic plot; indeed, she is quick to involve herself as an agent of the conspiracy: 'The image of it gives me content already, and I trust it will grow to a most prosperous perfection' (III.1.260–261). However, we cannot wipe out the level of our response to her refusal to allow Angelo to have his way.

Productions whose final impression is a statement about Isabella make it hard work for an audience who may see the issues as ones which go beyond the behaviour of individual characters. There are several topics which could make a fair claim to being central to *Measure for Measure*, but in order to illustrate the relationship between character and issue there is no need to go beyond two, law and virtue.

When Angelo is given the authority 'So to enforce or qualify the laws/ As to your soul seems good' (I.1.65–66), there is nothing in the scene to indicate what sort of code and what sort of society we are dealing with. When the Duke goes on in I.3 to explain to Friar Thomas that the purpose of the law is necessarily restraint, 'The needful bits and curbs to headstrong weeds' (line 20) — amended rather more convincingly to 'headstrong jades' in the Arden edition — and talks of the law as an instrument of vigorous education, 'the threatening twigs of birch' (line 24), we could well be in a society of cannibals where the tribal elders are deploring a new-fangled tendency to vegetarianism among the young people. 'The baby beats the nurse, and quite athwart/ Goes all decorum' (lines 30–31) has no moral imperative beyond the maintenance of an undefined status quo.

The questions which are raised go beyond the simple one of 'What should be lawful and what unlawful?' Pompey is quite capable of that level of argument in his exchange with Escalus:

> ESCALUS ... What do you think of the trade, Pompey? Is it a lawful trade?
> POMPEY If the law would allow it, sir.

(II.1.214–216)

The low life introduced by Lucio and the two Gentlemen also acknowledges law, in this case the Ten Commandments:

> LUCIO Thou conclud'st like the sanctimonious pirate, that went to sea with the Ten Commandments, but scraped one out of the table.
> SECOND GENTLEMAN 'Thou shalt not steal'?
> LUCIO Ay, that he razed.

(I.2.7–11)

Lucio, who already knows why Claudio has been arrested, offers 'murder' (I.2.136) as an example of shameful crime, but there can be few societies whose laws have not forbidden murder. There is not much to be gained from looking in *Measure for Measure* for an examination of what should be lawful. The wider issue which is raised is the need for law, the way in which a social group wants the security of such a code, and regards the fact that there *is* such a code as of more importance than what the code forbids. Escalus is moved to fury by the disguised Duke's suggestion that 'The Duke's unjust' (V.1.298), and threatens immediate torture. People who deny the effectiveness of the law:

> Laws for all faults,
> But faults so countenanced that the strong statutes
> Stand like the forfeits in a barber's shop,
> As much in mock as mark.

(V.1.317–320)

are to be hauled away to prison for speaking 'Slander to th'state' (line 321). There is no spirit of anarchy in Pompey or Lucio: 'If imprisonment be the due of a bawd, why, 'tis his right' (III.2.63–64). Their conduct only suggests the possibility of changing the laws. It is in Barnardine that we recognise that it is voluntary subjugation to rules on the part of the vast majority which allows authorities to keep their place. Barnardine, 'A man that apprehends death no more dreadfully but as a drunken sleep; careless, reckless, and fearless of what's past, present, or to come' (IV.2.139–141), is beyond law because there is nothing with which authority can threaten him to make him obedient. This is an opening to a form of freedom. In even the bleakest of contexts, the slave labour camps of the Gulag Archipelago, Solzhenitsyn describes the freedom some prisoners achieve through reconciling themselves to demeaning brutality:

> If it is the essence that counts, then the time has come to reconcile yourself to *general work*. To tatters. To torn skin on the hands. To a piece of bread which is smaller or worse. And perhaps . . . to death. But while you're alive, you drag yourself along proudly with an aching back. And that is when — when you have ceased to be afraid of threats and are not chasing after rewards — you become the most dangerous character in the owl-like view of the bosses. Because . . . what hold do they have on you?[2]

Barnardine is similarly dangerous, although his behaviour is perhaps closer to that of prisoners who go on a 'dirty protest', and who reduce their living conditions to such a state that there is no further punishment for them open to the authorities.

This glance at the idea of law in the play is enough to show that the issues go far beyond what can be compassed by a theatrical 'statement'. The same applies to virtue. Definitions are couched entirely in terms of absence and denial. Angelo is defined in negative terms, 'A man of stricture and firm absti-nence' (I.3.12). From what is he abstaining? Lucio sees Isabella as 'a thing enskied and sainted,/ By your renouncement, an immortal spirit' (I.4.34–35) (the punctuation in the Arden edition, 'a thing enskied and sainted/ By your renouncement, an immortal spirit' gives 'renouncement' even more force). While it may be simple enough to see this as a pointer to a positive embracing of life as a greater good, the text cannot be made to

---

[2] Alexander Solzhenitsyn, *The Gulag Archipelago*, Vol. 2, translated from the Russian by Thomas P Whitney (Glasgow, 1975), part IV, Chapter 1.

support quite so simple a reading. What is virtuous remains elusive, and the only altruistic act which is ever mentioned is Mistress Overdone's claim to have looked after Kate Keepdown's and Lucio's child for the last year and a quarter (III.2.190–194).

It is in terms of law — including that of property — and virtue that the all-pervading examination of sexuality is conducted. The Duke's self-consciousness on the topic indicates its inescapability. Try to construct the two speeches which have preceded his statement to Friar Thomas:

> No, holy father, throw away that thought;
> Believe not that the dribbling dart of love
> Can pierce a complete bosom. Why I desire thee
> To give me secret harbour hath a purpose
> More grave and wrinkled than the aims and ends
> Of burning youth.
>
> (I.3.1–6)

The Duke's request for a 'secret harbour' has clearly prompted immediate suspicions from the Friar, and the denial has more than a hint of over-emphasis. In the same way he answers the Provost's hesitations about leaving him alone with Isabella: 'My mind promises with my habit no loss shall touch her by my company' (III.1.179–180).

A reading which attempts to analyse the Duke's character while disregarding his dramatic function is bound to stress the importance of Isabella's final response to him. It is also a reading which will lose itself in contradictions; for example, can one imagine what would be the effect if Abhorson and Pompey managed to carry out the Duke's command about Barnardine, 'After him fellows, bring him to the block' (IV.3.63)? However, an examination of the nature of the demands made on the audience through the course of the play can lead to a resolution where Isabella's actions (or lack of action) can be relatively unimportant without diluting the powerful issues the text raises.

Although the idea of comic structure has already been mentioned, what is more important in *Measure for Measure* is the nature of response prompted in the audience. This is not a matter of like or dislike, approval or disapproval, but of whether we are being prompted to engage our emotions – to sympathise or to detest — or our intellects — to judge. Where these responses are most clearly called for is in the monologues and the asides to the audience, the moments when either the social defences are down or the character is openly trying to manipulate us. There are fifteen of these speeches, besides other moments when the second character on stage is being used as a bridge between the speaker and the audience. Although the first occasion is Mistress Overdone's brief lament (I.2.81–83) which invites laughter, the next is a 'bridge' speech when the final lines of what the Duke says to Friar Thomas (I.3.50–54), already quoted above, draw us into the world of plot, a world where we are invited to distance ourselves from Angelo and act as observers, judging him as a potential 'seemer'.

Both of these speeches show an awareness of the audience; indeed, they may be delivered directly at us. The next four — II.2.141–142; II.2.161–187; II.4.1–17; and II.4.19–30 — reveal a profound sense of privacy. Angelo, the speaker on each occasion, is exploring his sensations with horrified fascination. We are eavesdroppers, and the immediate appeal is emotional. We may sympathise, we may be revolted, but the initial response is not to stand back and judge. The horror and the fascination can be seen in the way he tries to approach the topic in generalised terms, 'our sense' (II.2.169). 'Shall we desire' (line 171) and 'our evils' (line 172) attempt to keep his mind and his feelings apart in his questioning, 'What dost thou? Or what art thou, Angelo?' (line 173), but he eventually faces the unique nature of his desire: 'this virtuous maid/ Subdues me quite' (lines 185–186). His next two monologues, an attempt to come to terms with this desire as the second meeting with Isabella approaches, are intensely private. Indeed, he lets slip mention of 'my gravity,/ Wherein, let no man hear me, I take pride' (II.4.9–10). This is not a shared moment with us. Angelo is totally vulnerable as he explores himself in front of us, and the plane on which we respond is the emotional, the world of tragedy.

Isabella's only monologue (II.4.171–187) is the next, and her potential helplessness, 'To whom should I complain?' (line 171) leaves her with no choice but to spell out her principles. (Though it is possible to imagine a reading which sees the whole speech as an attempt to persuade herself of the necessity of 'Isabel, live chaste, and, brother, die' (line 184).) Our response is in the same terms as our one to Angelo, even if the depth of sympathy is different.

Angelo has one further monologue, the last in the play (IV.4.18–32), which is the same in nature as his others. But in the meantime we have been prompted to a different nature of response by a further eight monologues, seven from the Duke and one from Pompey. These invite us to ponder the absurdity of our attempts to preserve our dignity, to distance ourselves from the emotional response, and to realise that laughter is the only sane response to predicaments which we cannot control. 'No might nor greatness in mortality/ Can censure 'scape (III.2.175–176), observes the Duke directly to us. Dignity is no protection. Angelo's 'gravity' in which he takes secret pride makes him the more vulnerable. Whatever man may 'within him hide' (III.2.259), it will out, and the Duke shares his plan with us: 'Craft against vice I must apply' (line 265). There is no escape, not for all the rakes and men-about-town whom Pompey rediscovers in prison (IV.3.1–18), nor for *anyone*, however virtuous:

> O place and greatness, millions of false eyes
> Are stuck upon thee. Volumes of report
> Run with these false and most contrarious quests
> Upon thy doings; thousand escapes of wit
> Make thee the father of their idle dream,
> And rack thee in their fancies.

(IV.1.59–64)

It is not so much the structure of the plot but the nature of our responses which creates the sense of comedy at the end. The 'thousand escapes of wit' do not necessarily signal frivolity. It can take more courage to embrace one's absurdity than to attempt to cling to dignity. Angelo's reaction when exposed is to beg for instant death. This would be the most satisfying conclusion for him because it avoids any kind of self-assessment, the application of reason which reveals his pretensions as absurd. Laughter is crueller than sympathy, and Angelo begs for the sympathetic response. This is in obvious contrast with Lucio who manages to fulfil his ambition to 'speak so wisely under an arrest' (I.2.130), when he abandons any attempt to appear dignified: 'If you will hang me for it, you may. But I had rather it would please you I might be whipped' (V.1.502–503).

Isabella is not just the area where the three elements of the plot meet, she is also an integral part of the aspects of the play which demand an emotional response, and of those parts which require detached intelligence. The theatrical tradition from which Shakespeare's plays were freeing themselves was that of overt didacticism, of the ending making an unambiguous moral judgement with which the audience could be expected to agree. Of course, Isabella has to do *something* in the closing moments, but for her action to be a clear comment and judgement on the play is to relegate one whole range of our responses to a level of secondary importance.

AFTERTHOUGHTS

1

Why does Saunders argue that 'it does not really matter what Isabella does' at the end of the play (page 87)? Do you agree?

2

Which — if any — of the suggested interpretations of Isabella's refusal to sleep with Angelo (page 88) do you favour?

3

Do you agree that in *Measure for Measure* 'what is virtuous remains elusive' (page 92)?

4

Do you find that your own response to the play is predominantly emotional or predominantly intellectual?

John E Cunningham

John E Cunningham currently divides his time between writing and travel. He is the author of numerous critical studies.

ESSAY

Tickling commodity

Since in suburban England no one is ever more than three metres from a TV set, we are all familiar with old gangster movies and the way in which a former American code of censorship produced these highly ambiguous stories whose villains are shown to enjoy an exciting life — fast cars, fast women, fast bucks — and only in the last reel are 'punished', either shot by G-men as vicious as themselves, or dourly led off by cloned cops; probably, we suspect, to get off on a legal quibble discovered by an expensive lawyer. Villainy, at a safe distance, is always attractive and virtue is dull. Shakespeare had to cope with this ambivalence: his Falstaff almost steals two plays, only to be given his necessary come-uppance at the very end; many actors will fight shy of the role of Othello but leap at Iago's far more interesting part. Yet Shakespeare had his Hays Office of censorship too in the Puritans, powerful in the City, who would gladly have closed him down on the grounds that plays glamorised and encouraged wickedness.

A superficial reading of *Measure for Measure* might indeed suggest that that is what he was doing — worse, leading characters engage in 'immorality', and in the end get away with it. Isabella has a thankless part to play in her armour-plated chastity. Indeed, casual, blasé, modern readers or spectators are inclined to blame her for not shutting her eyes, opening her defences and saving her brother, as she did in the original story that Shakespeare — significantly — altered. Lucio is very funny onstage and makes the Duke seem stuffy by comparison. Mistress Overdone appears to be one of a long line of moral imbeciles — Juliet's Nurse, Mistress Quickly — at whom we laugh without condemnation. The law, talked of so much in this play, is the usual ass, condemning in Claudio what is deliberately encouraged as the righting of a wrong between Angelo and Mariana.

We may begin our own exploration by looking at some of the play's attitudes to the law, supposed to be the codified morality of a society. There are three exemplars, apart from an anonymous Justice who gets invited to dinner: the Duke, Angelo and Escalus.

The Duke has been negligent in sustaining the rule of law, and dispenses it only at the end; Angelo is at first over-zealous to press it to the uttermost letter, then uses the power it gives him for selfish ends; but the first person we see in the everyday task of administering it is Escalus. At the beginning of the second Act, before trying to wade his way through Elbow's evidence about Pompey, Escalus has an argument with Angelo about the condemnation of Claudio. He urges clemency:

> Let us be keen and rather cut a little
> Than fall, and bruise to death

(II.1.5–6)

and he goes on to suggest two reasons for such restraint, apart from the genial notion that moderation is desirable in itself: one is that Claudio 'had a most noble father', a reason then perhaps more acceptable than now, though always unsound; and second, a point he makes at length, that if Angelo himself had ever been in the right — or wrong — circumstances, he might well have done the same thing as Claudio. Angelo readily admits that those who administer justice may themselves be culpable, but says — surely correctly — that this does not invalidate the process:

> I not deny,
> The jury, passing on the prisoner's life
> May in the sworn twelve have a thief or two
> Guiltier than him they try

(II.1.18–21)

He ends, however, by imputing to himself, as well as to the law, infallibility. If ever he offends in the same way, he is to be judged by his own rule. The law, to him, is absolute.

Just as he obviously believes himself immune to ordinary temptation, he is also immune to absurdity: it is a serious matter to lack a sense of humour, and he soon grows impatient of Elbow's ramblings and leaves the carrying out of justice to Escalus. This Escalus does badly, partly because *his* sense of humour is too easily tickled. Pompey amuses him and so he lets him off. But there is a serious point discussed between them:

> ESCALUS How would you live Pompey? By being a bawd? What do you think of the trade, Pompey? Is it a lawful trade?
>
> POMPEY If the law would allow it, sir.
>
> ESCALUS But the law will not allow it, Pompey; nor it shall not be allowed in Vienna.
>
> POMPEY Does your worship mean to geld and splay all the youth of the city?
>
> (II.1.213–220)

Escalus shies away from this issue, one that modern law has tackled no more honestly than that of seventeenth-century Vienna: don't punish the traders but stop the customers, and there will be no trade. Instead, Escalus makes a few jokes about Pompey's first name — he has already been heavily facetious about his last one — and lets him off with a caution, which Pompey tells us he will ignore. Back he goes to his unsavoury business: 'I shall follow it', he says, 'as the flesh and fortune shall better determine' (II.1.241–242). Pompey lives for the day. It was not a long day for his livestock. When Lucio asks after Mistress Overdone, he is told:

> Troth, sir, she hath eaten up all her beef, and she is herself in the tub
>
> (III.2.53–54)

a chilling reference to the casualty rate and cure — which was no cure, merely a way of suppressing symptoms — for syphilis. That this was endemic amongst her customers, the young riff-raff of Vienna, we have already been told: some of Mistress Overdone's regulars make gruesome fun of each other's venereal disasters:

> Thou art good velvet. Thou'rt a three-piled piece, I warrant thee.
> I had as lief be a list of an English kersey as be piled, as thou art
> piled, for a French velvet. Do I speak feelingly now?
>
> (I.2.31–35)

says one of them to Lucio, referring to the loss of hair in the later stages of what was called the French disease. And there is much more ribbing on the same dreary theme. As we listen, we begin to wonder what sort of a future any of these people can look forward to: the suggestion, at the beginning of the scene, that they are all soldiers eager for the excitement of war perhaps partly explains their way of living totally in the present.

Lucio, the amusing Lucio, is unable to resist any immediate temptation to be funny, to have his joke: he will do it with a stranger, he will do it at the point of death. Talking to a supposed wandering friar, he cannot help but pretend to close knowledge of the Duke to make an effect, accusing him of shocking promiscuity: 'Yes, your beggar of fifty, and his use was to put a ducat in her clack-dish' (III.2.119–120). When that friar stands revealed as the slandered Duke and condemns him to marry, he must still have his joke:

> Marrying a punk, my lord, is pressing to death, whipping, and
> hanging.
>
> (V.1.519–520)

The Duke says briefly that 'slandering a prince deserves it' — in contemporary thought the whole force of the law resided in the person of the monarch; but Lucio is not made to answer for that. What he *is* forced to do at the end of the play is to accept personal responsibility for what he personally has done, and of which he had actually boasted to the Duke:

> DUKE   Did you do such a thing? [*as seduce a girl on promise of
>   marriage*]
> LUCIO   Yes, marry, did I, but I was fain to forswear it. They
>   would else have married me to the rotten medlar.
>
> (IV.3.168–170)

In the same way, Claudio is told:

> She, Claudio, that you wronged, look you restore
>
> (V.1.522)

and Angelo has already been forced to marry the ill-treated Mariana whom he had long ago abandoned. Above all, in this final scene, the Duke himself takes full responsibility in his own person for the situation in Vienna — a product partly of his own laxness, partly of his appointing such a deputy — and for the various plots he has laid; even the bewildered, well-meaning Provost is remembered and rewarded at the end.

And Isabella, to the displeasure of some critics, is offered a ducal marriage! We shall see that there is ample scope in the movement of the drama for a highly dependent and trusting relationship between her and the friar to develop, with the promise of more; but how does Isabella, supposedly so clear in her beliefs, fit into a pattern that is beginning to emerge, that of the conflict between self-interest and opportunism on the one hand, and accepting our responsibilities on the other?

What Shakespeare thought about conventual existence we do not know for certain, though there is a striking passage in *A Midsummer Night's Dream* about 'withering on the virgin thorn' (I.1.77) which sounds discouraging. When the beautiful Isabella is first presented to us complaining that 'the votarists of Saint Clare' have not a severe enough rule for her, most of us will feel uneasy at such an austere view of life in one so young and of unknown potential. Moreover, a set of rules — and those of the Clares were strict enough for most people — is in a sense a way of avoiding the making of moral choices, since these are all made for us if we absolutely accept — as a nun must — what the rules impose. It is an important part of Isabella's education in the world to which she seems likely to return at the end of the play, that she learns to look at rules and collate them with her own inclinations, both good and bad. She says of Claudio's sin:

> There is a vice that most I do abhor,
> And most desire should meet the blow of justice,
> For which I would not plead, but that I must,
> For which I must not plead, but that I am
> At war 'twixt will and will not.

> (II.2.29–33)

Her (good) inclination here is to save her brother if she can, and she goes on to press her case with considerable forensic skill against an able advocate and one who holds all the official right on his side. In particular she urges the grace — a word of theological import here, perhaps — of mercy, a theme Shakespeare made central to another play, *The Merchant of Venice*, where the letter of the law is insisted on, then turned against the man who presses it, so that he is spared only by the exercise of the compassion he had refused to show.

At the end of the play, a man whose power is greater than Angelo's tempts Isabella to acquiesce in the normal pattern of the law, a death for a death; the Duke, still maintaining the fiction of Claudio's execution, tells Mariana when she tries to enlist Isabella to her cause:

> Against all sense you do importune her.
> Should she kneel down in mercy of this fact,
> Her brother's ghost his pavèd bed would break,
> And take her hence in horror.

(V.1.430–433)

The word 'sense' here is ambiguous: not only sense of justice, sense of what is due to family honour, but also 'feeling' is implied — her natural antipathy towards Angelo, who has apparently killed her brother, tried to whore her and broken his promise. Isabella pleads:

> I partly think
> A due sincerity governed his deeds
> Till he did look on me

(V.1.442–444)

for which critics who dislike her accuse her of coyness; but she speaks the plain truth of what happened. And she goes on to argue that her brother did at least commit the wrong for which he was condemned, Angelo only meant to, and we are not to be condemned for mere intentions — which is just as well for all of us.

Isabella has come a long way from the austere postulant of her earlier scenes, and it is possible to look at her various experiences — with Lucio, with her own brother who so unexpectedly betrays her trust in him, with the friar to whom she turns as a natural figure of authority, with Mariana, a model of duty and devotion to a less than deserving man — as a process of education in the temporal world. At the end of it she has learned to see the rules as made for man, and to assert the validity of her own moral judgement, however hard it is on her own natural feelings.

Opportunism, also, she has learned, can rebound on those who pursue it. When Angelo first makes his infamous proposition to her, she at once believes she has the advantage of him, and snatches at it:

> I will proclaim thee, Angelo, look for't!
> Sign me a present pardon for my brother,
> Or with an outstretched throat I'll tell the world
> What man thou art.
>
> (II.4.151–154)

Though this is in a good enough cause, it is blackmail, and Angelo chillingly rebuffs her, first by pointing out that no one will believe her, then:

> Say what you can, my false o'erweighs your true
>
> (II.4.170)

— perhaps a way of saying that she has been trying — and failing — to play him at his own game.

This is at the end of a speech in which Angelo shows opportunism at its most repellent. Having, as he thinks, a helpless person in front of him, he tells her in plain terms that she must not only surrender herself to him, but must submit herself to his every sexual whim:

> I have begun,
> And now I give my sensual race the rein.
> Fit thy consent to my sharp appetite,
> Lay by all nicety and prolixious blushes,
> That banish what they sue for. Redeem thy brother
> By yielding up thy body to my will,
> Or else he must not only die the death,
> But thy unkindness shall his death draw out
> To lingering sufferance.
>
> (II.4.159–167)

Earlier he has said that professional women with all their tricks could never move him, and has asked himself if he desires her 'foully for those things/ That make her good' (II.2.174–175).

What is happening to Angelo is a good deal more than those unhappy late-arising impulses which land a number of bewildered elderly gentlemen in court on rather lesser charges: he is a deeply repressed man in whom represssion has bred downright cruelty and a perverse desire to foul what is pure; the probable basis for what we sometimes call the corruption of minors. This is to impose a modern vocabulary on a character created before that vocabulary existed; Angelo would probably have been seen by contemporaries as a sketch of a type of Puritan — but his urges and motivation would have been well understood. He is also a man who has always lived by the rules — by the rules and nothing else, by the law which must never be made a scarecrow (even if it is bad law?). He has lived, in other words, as Isabella had wanted to live in the future: by the book. How little that book means to him when it runs counter to his deep desires is plain. He abandons every sense of prudence to seize the moment; worse, to break his sorry bargain, for he orders Claudio's death despite Isabella's apparent acquiescence. Everything is subordinated to the ferocious urgings of the moment — for a rational man as he normally is, could not hope to go on indefinitely suppressing evidence, killing the inconvenient; but the remorseless exponential imperative of tyranny goads him on.

But Angelo, whose blood is very snow-broth, does not stay now to consider this. He acts with no more forethought than was shown by the syphilitic customers of Madam Mitigation whose girls do for money what Claudio, for one horrifying moment, wants his sister to do for love of him; with no more sense of his responsibility than Lucio showed to Kate when he got her with child on a promise of marriage afterwards forsworn; with no more care for anyone than that same Lucio shows to his old friend Pompey when he falls on hard times and asks for bail; with no more heed of his immortal soul — in which, of course, Shakespeare implicitly believed — than Barnardine has, roaring drunk in the shadow of the axe. It is often observed that Shakespeare's plays could be supposed to take place almost anywhere — that there is no difference between the Athens of *A Midsummer Night's Dream* and the Messina of *Much Ado*: but the Vienna of this play does acquire a life of its own, and a pretty unsavoury life it is too: a life where so many people, amusing as they sometimes are, seem to live now and vaguely hope they will not have to pay later.

It is this corrupt and decadent city, which the Duke has too casually ruled for too long, that he sets out to explore in a disguise that will give him the entrée to any place and any heart; for the Duke too may be seen as part of the moral framework we have been suggesting. In his opening scene he says:

> I love the people,
> But do not like to stage me to their eyes;
> Though it do well, I do not relish well
> Their loud applause and aves vehement,
> Nor do I think the man of safe discretion
> That does affect it

(I.1.67–72)

— this last justification perhaps a sop to the court, before whom this play was given, of James I, whose dislike of mixing with his people was notorious. But a monarch of those times had a duty to be seen as a ruler — Elizabeth had always understood this — as well as to be seen as a possible source of clemency to lesser men. The Duke sets out to achieve for himself what comes by hard experience to those other characters who are not incorrigible: personal responsibility.

A ruler had another duty too, and one in which Elizabeth played a delaying game all her life, arguably with disastrous long-term consequences: to marry and provide continuity for the throne. Though this last act of the Duke's — his implied proposal of marriage to Isabella — has been much derided as a mere happy ending, it is surely a perfectly proper conclusion to his assumption of all the obligations of his role, as well as being far from improbable in human terms: we have only to see how much Isabella has come to turn to him for help, support and guidance in, for example, the business of the plot concerning Mariana.

And what of those characters who are not incorrigible? Lucio will never learn, but we all love a rogue if he has amused us, and the Duke — or more correctly, the Duke's creator, a hard-headed impresario — lets him off with a wife to keep him, perhaps, in order of a sort; Mariana, the most selfless and devoted of lovers, may do as much for Angelo. Claudio is to be a husband and father — as he always intended. Isabella is to return to the world she would have renounced for a rule-book. The cast takes its bow and we, the audience of cheerfully improvident mortals, go about our business of the day.

AFTERTHOUGHTS

1

Is wickedness either 'glamorised' or 'encouraged' in *Measure for Measure* (page 97)?

2

Do you agree that Escalus dispenses justice 'badly' (page 99)?

3

In what ways, according to Cunningham, has Isabella undergone 'a process of education in the temporal world' (pages 102)? Are you convinced?

4

Do you agree that the Duke's proposal of marriage to Isabella is a 'perfectly proper conclusion' (page 105)?

Diana Devlin

Diana Devlin has taught Theatre Arts and directed extensively in colleges and universities in Great Britain and the USA. She is a director of the Shakespeare Globe Project, and now works at Leeds Castle in Kent.

ESSAY

'To veil full purpose': revelation and response in the final Act

The final Act of *Measure for Measure* resembles a classic English whodunit where a famous detective gathers suspects together and triumphantly uncovers the murderer. The Duke Vincentio deliberately arranges that all the relevant people are present at the city gates, so that Angelo's crime can be revealed. Unlike the readers of a whodunit, the audience already knows what he has done. The important thing is that the truth is discovered to the characters and the crime dealt with effectively. An additional slant is provided by the Duke's involvement. A detective is pulled in after the crime is committed, and investigates by looking for clues to what occurred, but the Duke has actually witnessed and contrived some of the events. The extent of his involvement is also discovered, including his suddenly expressed wish to marry Isabella. The scene is essentially a series of revelatory statements, including confessions and judicial pronouncements. But, strangely, the play ends with the one important pronouncement unstated. When the Duke proposes marriage to Isabella, no speech is ascribed to her in response. At the end of the play we do not know from the script whether she goes with him, and if she does, whether she goes willingly; or whether, instead, she returns to the strict rule of the convent. I propose to examine the Act in some detail to see what significance can be placed upon his proposal and her unspoken response to it.

The scene brings together three plots on which the whole play has been based. One of these plots derives from a story Shakespeare probably knew, in which a young woman is forced to sleep with a corrupt magistrate for the same reason that Isabella is pressured to sleep with Angelo. In this story, (contained in the *Hecatommithi* of Giraldo Cinthio), the young woman appeals to the emperor for justice. The emperor marries her to the magistrate, then condemns him to death, but she pleads for his life. Thus, justice is balanced with clemency. Shakespeare has complicated this story by adding a plot twist in the form of the bed-trick, so that Angelo has not in fact slept with Isabella. But he constructs the last scene in such a way that Isabella, like the young woman in the story, faces a moral dilemma where she must choose between justice and clemency.

The third plot element is the one which sets the whole framework for the play, and for the final Act in particular. It is the situation of the ruler who disguises himself to go amongst his people and find out the truth. Shakespeare had used this plot device himself in *Henry V*, where the king goes round the soldiers' camp the night before the battle of Agincourt. In that play, the situation not only reveals the people's thoughts and feelings to the king, but also reveals his vulnerability to the audience. In considering the final Act of *Measure for Measure*, we should ask ourselves how much of the truth about himself the Duke reveals both to the other characters and to the audience.

The scene opens with the formal greetings between the Duke and the magistrates, Angelo and Escalus. His speech is completely false as it relates to Angelo, for he tells him he has heard 'Such goodness of your justice' (V.1.6) that he must give him public thanks. Angelo replies, 'You make my bonds still greater' (line 8), overtly the answer of a loyal, grateful subject, but carrying a hidden truth since he is like a prisoner, bound by the knowledge he has committed a sin. The Duke, knowing the hidden truth, presses it on Angelo, by assuring him 'O, your deserts speak loud' (line 9), and by insisting that Angelo walk publicly beside him so that the citizens know:

> That outward courtesies would fain proclaim
> Favours that keep within.

(line 15–16)

The Duke's approach is to put on a 'show' that all is well, presumably in an attempt to force Angelo to some confession. The more he flatters, the more the truth of Angelo's 'deserving' glares. But Angelo remains silent, and a dumb show ensues as the Duke parades with his magistrates by his side, a false picture of good government.

Now comes the next part of the Duke's production, in clear imitation of Cinthio's story. As instructed by false and true friars ('Friar Lodowick', the disguised Duke, and his accomplice Friar Peter), Isabella calls on the Duke for justice, and tells the full story, not as it happened, but as Angelo thinks it happened; that is, he tempted her, she yielded to him but he still sent Claudio to his death. She has previously told Mariana how much she dislikes this ruse:

> To speak so indirectly I am loath.
> I would say the truth . . .

(IV.6.1–2)

But the 'Friar'/Duke advised her to do it 'to veil full purpose' (IV.6.4), and so she does, pleading for justice against Angelo. After only two attempts to stop her, Angelo is silent, and stands by while Isabella tries to tear his mask off.

Now the role the Duke is playing reaches its greatest complexity. As Duke, he pretends to disbelieve Isabella, commenting sarcastically, 'This is most likely!' (V.1.103), and accusing her of having been 'prompted', which of course she has. He tells her:

> Confess the truth, and say by whose advice
> Thou cam'st here to complain.

(line 113–114)

Temporarily, he thus betrays Isabella, trapping her in the mixture of truth and untruth she has allowed herself to be entangled in. She prepares to leave, saying with troubled dignity:

> Heaven shield your grace from woe,
> As I thus wrongèd hence unbelievèd go.

(line 118–119)

When pressed again, she tells him of Friar Lodowick, whom Lucio at once accuses of being 'a meddling friar'. The joke against Lucio begins to build up, as he flatters the Duke, protects himself and lets his tongue lead him into the trap being laid for him. But meanwhile, Friar Peter's next speech falsely clears both Friar Lodowick ('I know him for a man divine and holy', line 144) and Angelo ('this worthy nobleman', 159), thus mingling true and false no less confusingly than Lucio.

The 'show' proceeds; at this point, action speaks more powerfully than the rhetoric of true and false. Isabella is led off, guarded, believing that the Duke has failed as a purveyor of justice, while Angelo remains silent, believing he has got away with his crimes. Mariana is brought on. She explains her situation, the first character to speak the truth in this scene, but it is a riddling truth and she is veiled.

> My lord, I do confess I ne'er was married,
> And I confess besides I am no maid;
> I have known my husband, yet my husband
> Knows not that ever he knew me.

(line 184–187)

The Duke, Mariana and the audience are all in cahoots. Mysterious as the sphinx, Mariana proceeds to elaborate on the enigma, drawing Angelo at last into speech, as he searches, like Oedipus, for the answer to the riddles that may actually seal his doom. 'Charges she more than me?' (line 198) he asks heavily. The suspense is kept high as she continues to give all her answers indirectly, up to the moment when she finally unveils, and explains the bed-trick to Angelo's face.

At this point, Lucio interjects with one of his frequent comments, and is, as usual, snubbed by the Duke. The break in the flow of the Duke's created drama is enough to give Angelo a chance to recover himself. Suddenly, from dumbstruck silence he changes to the confident eloquence he had always shown until now. The Duke is forced to continue the false show beyond the moment he had planned. As Duke, he can do no more at this point. He hands over the reins to Escalus and quickly exits, to see how the presence of 'Friar Lodowick' can help the situation. It may well be that the Duke's later irritation and anger at Lucio is motivated by pride over this untimely interruption, which stops the denouement proceeding as he intended.

From this point on, the Duke is less in control. The situation reverts to the hit-and-miss state of justice we have seen in the rest of the play. Pomp and ceremony are dropped, verse is replaced by prose, except for the 'friar'/Duke who speaks in a more authoritative tone than before, accusing his alter ego:

> The Duke's unjust,
> Thus to retort your manifest appeal
> And put your trial in the Villain's mouth
> Which here you come to accuse.

> (line 298–301)

This rings true. Perhaps the double role he is playing makes him begin to see the wrong he did in leaving the city in the first place. But his accusation brings loyal Escalus's wrath upon him:

> We'll touse you
> Joint by joint, but we will know his purpose.
> What? Unjust?

> (line 309–311)

So threatened is the 'friar'/Duke's position, he has to call upon his true authority to protect it:

> The Duke
> Dare no more stretch this finger of mine than he
> Dare rack his own.

> (line 311–312)

This paradoxical line, instead of leading back into a role-playing game, frees him to speak more truthfully than he has done before. Liberated from his ducal role, he describes the real situation in the city:

> My business in this state
> Makes me a looker-on here in Vienna,

Where I have seen corruption boil and bubble
Till it o'errun the stew. Laws for all faults,
But faults so countenanced that the strong statutes
Stand like the forfeits in a barber's shop,
As much in mock as mark.

(line 314–320)

The 'disguised ruler' plot is coming to fruition, showing the audience that the Duke's opting-out was irresponsible. His motive in leaving Angelo to clear up the mess that 'fourteen years had let slip' was to avoid slander to himself, and to stand back and see what was really happening in Vienna. Now, returning again as the friar, he finds himself in difficulties, his word (quite correctly) not trusted. What, after all, is there to choose between a scheming, lying friar and a scheming lying Lucio?

DUKE I protest I love the Duke as I love myself.
ANGELO Hark, how the villain would close now, after his treasonable abuses.

(line 338–340)

When Escalus sends him to prison, the Provost, who knows the truth, has no option but to obey. Finally, it is Lucio's insolence, not the triumph of truth or justice, that breaks the deadlocked situation, as he tauntingly pulls off the friar's hood and reveals the Duke.

Prose is now dropped again for verse, and the Duke takes up his full reins of authority to confront his wretched deputy. Angelo sees a divinity in the Duke's omniscience:

. . . I perceive your grace, like power divine,
Hath looked upon my passes.

(line 366–367)

The Duke sustains the dignity and power of his office, as he proceeds, like the emperor in Cinthio's story, to send Angelo off to marry — not Isabella of course — but Mariana. Isabella now asks pardon for having 'employed and pained/ Your unknown sovereignty' (383–384). The Duke grants this pardon, but must surely lack credibility for the audience, as he then reverts to deception, explaining and comforting her for Claudio's death, which the audience knows did not take place. As Mariana and Angelo return, now married, he commands her to pardon Angelo for wronging her honour, but then condemns Angelo to death as recompense for Claudio's death.

The last piece of play-acting now moves towards its climax. The Duke sets out the justice of Angelo's punishment, but paradoxically links it with mercy:

> The very mercy of the law cries out
> Most audible, even from his proper tongue,
> 'An Angelo for Claudio, death for death!'

(line 404–406)

He goes on to draw other terms together which must be set against each other:

> Haste still pays haste, and leisure answers leisure,
> Like doth quit like, and Measure still for Measure.

(line 407–408)

The speech slows down his action from the frenzied pace of the friar's actions to the measured pace of a judge summing up a case. The words direct us towards a different view of justice than has been expressed earlier in the play. Here, justice is not the enactment of laws and statutes, but justice as equity (or fair treatment), a system of valuation, where deeds, not reputations, are set against each other, like debts and credits in an account, to balance perfectly. Although still enmeshed in one last lie, the Duke expresses here the meaning of true justice that he has discovered from his experiment in government. However, it is an abstract view, taking little account of the hurly-burly of the city streets, and the contingent quality of all that happens in human affairs.

Mariana now pleads for the life of her husband, but the Duke is adamant. Finally, she begs Isabella to plead with her, and the dramatic focus swings back to Isabella. Suspense is high, created by the playwright's skilful structuring of revelation, giving Isabella a true test of clemency, for she still believes her brother is dead. Since the Duke has earlier lost some of his control of the drama, we may question whether he is still the playwright here, manoeuvring her into the position of choice. He has taken great pains to disguise the truth about Claudio, but what game is he up to? If she does *not* plead for Angelo, what will he do? Claudio is alive, and therefore if 'Like doth quit like', then Angelo does not deserve to die.

The importance of this moment then, does not rest, as most of the characters think, in the fate of Angelo. Indeed, a few lines later he tells Escalus he would rather die. It rests in our view of Isabella. For her, the wheel has come full circle. She, a novitiate nun, now stands again before the highest authority, being asked to plead for the life of a man who has broken the law against fornication. The stage direction 'ISABELLA (*kneeling*)' says it all. Although, as a novice, she must spend much of her time in prayer, and although she has told the Duke that she knelt before Angelo, this is the first time in the play that she has knelt. At the same time, she addresses the Duke as 'Most bounteous sir' (line 440), for the first time taking us beyond the 'mercy of the law' to awaken thoughts of a larger, perhaps divine, mercy. She goes on:

> Look, if it please you, on this man condemned
> As if my brother lived.

(line 441–442)

To her, as to most of the other characters, Claudio's survival will seem miraculous. But to all, both characters and audience, Isabella's action itself appears miraculous. She, not the Duke, is demonstrating that higher level of mercy for which she pleads.

Following hard upon her gesture of graciousness comes the 'unmuffling' of Claudio. The great critic Samuel Johnson expressed surprise because, 'Isabel is not made to express either gratitude, wonder or joy at the sight of her brother' (note to V.1.490, New Penguin edition, p. 182). Instead, the Duke uses this very moment to pop the question to her! J M Nosworthy, editor of the New Penguin edition, supposes that this lack of reaction is explained by the line, 'But fitter time for that', and compares the moment with other comic endings when Shakespeare picks up speed towards the imminent conclusion. However, this is to gloss over the significance of the moment. There is an obvious parallel within the play. Once again, Isabella's brave challenge to authority is immediately followed by a sexual approach from that 'authority'. This is worth looking at.

Throughout the play, we have been asked to measure one man's sexual behaviour against another's: Claudio's virtuous intentions agains Lucio's lechery, both against Angelo's lust for Isabella, and all those against Angelo's 'virtuous', tricked act with Mariana. How are we, and how is Isabella, to measure the Duke's behaviour, remembering especially that for most of the play he has appeared to her in the guise of a friar? His proposal not only changes their present relationship, it must also reflect back on his earlier behaviour. 'Friar Lodowick's' intervention in Claudio's case, we (and Isabella) may now suspect, was not the pure, impartial interest it was taken to be, but was motivated by an attraction towards Isabella. Angelo was first attracted by Isabella's eloquence and virtue. ('She speaks, and 'tis/ Such sense that my sense breeds with it', II.2.141–142, and 'Can it be/ That modesty may more betray our sense/ Than woman's lightness?', II.2.168–170). If the Duke is attracted by the same qualities, then it is not surprising that her speech begging for Angelo's life should finally convince him that she is the woman for him. In this union, justice and clemency would meet. But also, as in some ribald comic strip, the friar would couple with the nun. Isabella's silence leaves her own response in doubt, and keeps the Duke's behaviour and motivation ambiguous, since he is never questioned about it. Her last words have been strangely prophetic of the doubtful situation in which she leaves the audience, and, perhaps, the Duke, 'Thoughts are no subjects,/ Intents but merely thoughts' (V.1.450–451).

In Shakespeare's *The Winter's Tale*, a character is restored to life in a quasi-miraculous fashion which suggests some beneficent force governing human destiny. But in *Measure for Measure* he makes a more cynical statement, by continually reminding the audience of the wiles, deceits and trickery that pepper the conduct of human affairs, especially where sex is concerned, even for those who have good intentions.

It is fitting that the last character the Duke must deal with is Lucio:

> You, sirrah, that knew me for a fool, a coward,
> One all of luxury, an ass, a madman,
> Wherein have I so deserved of you,
> That you extol me thus?

(line 497–500)

Lucio would best reply by turning to the audience for support, for they have certainly witnessed the Duke to be some of these things — a fool to trust Angelo, a coward to abrogate his authority, and something like a madman in his sometimes frenetic role-changing. He has exploited his true position, indulged in trickery and intrigue, skulked in dark corners. The final exchange between them, when Lucio has been pardoned from death but condemned to marry a prostitute, is both comic and bitter. 'Marrying a punk, my lord, is pressing to death, whipping, and hanging,' laments Lucio, perhaps thinking of the diseases he may catch. 'Slandering a prince deserves it,' retorts the Duke, secure in his authority, which he proceeds to exercise fully in this last speech, where he gives his final commands and confirms his wish to marry Isabella. Will she accept him, or return to her convent? Read the next exciting instalment!

The pairing-off of all the couples, typical of Shakespeare's comic endings, suggests that she will marry the Duke as a true resolution of the drama, but her silence, and the volatile role-changing character of the Duke, throws a veil of secrecy over the kind of marriage they will have, and over her view of his authority, both as a ruler and as a husband.

When she was first confronted with Angelo's tyranny, Isabella's anger moved her to cry out against more than Angelo, to take in the whole of his sex, or indeed the whole of humanity:

> . . . man, proud man,
> Dressed in a little brief authority,
> Most ignorant of what he's most assured,
> His glassy essence, like an angry ape
> Plays such fantastic tricks before high heaven
> As makes the angels weep; who with our spleens,
> Would all themselves laugh mortal.

(II.2.117–123)

The Duke fits this picture. I should like to think that finally Isabella accepts her own mortality — first, by including herself in the term 'man, proud man', for she too has played 'fantastic tricks' with her sophistical arguments and moralising; and second, by recognising that, as a mortal, she may laugh instead of weep. The Duke has played a glorious practical joke in hiding Claudio's survival from her. She should enjoy the laugh against herself, and let the friar run off with the nun.

AFTERTHOUGHTS

1

What does Devlin suggest to be the meaning of 'true justice' (page 114)? Do you agree?

2

How do you respond to Isabella's action in pleading for Angelo's life (page 115)?

3

Do you agree with Devlin's suggestion as to what prompts the Duke's proposal (page 116)?

4

Do you agree with the closing statement of this essay?

A PRACTICAL GUIDE TO ESSAY WRITING

INTRODUCTION

First, a word of warning. Good essays are the product of a creative engagement with literature. So never try to restrict your studies to what you think will be 'useful in the exam'. Ironically, you will restrict your grade potential if you do.

This doesn't mean, of course, that you should ignore the basic skills of essay writing. When you read critics, make a conscious effort to notice *how* they communicate their ideas. The guidelines that follow offer advice of a more explicit kind. But they are no substitute for practical experience. It is never easy to express ideas with clarity and precision. But the more often you tackle the problems involved and experiment to find your own voice, the more fluent you will become. So practise writing essays as often as possible.

HOW TO PLAN
AN ESSAY

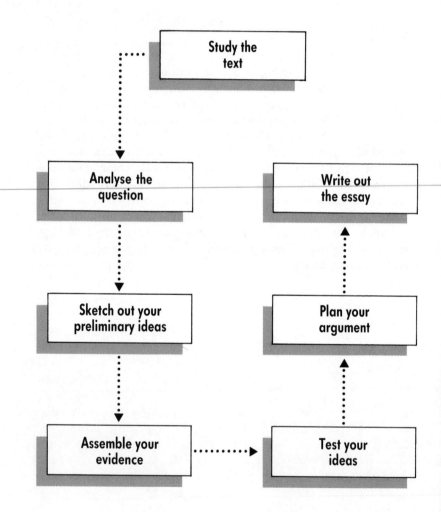

Study the text

The first step in writing a good essay is to get to know the set text well. Never write about a text until you are fully familiar with it. Even a discussion of the opening chapter of a novel, for example, should be informed by an understanding of the book as a whole. Literary texts, however, are by their very nature complex and on a first reading you are bound to miss many significant features. Re-read the book with care, if possible more than once. Look up any unfamiliar words in a good dictionary and if the text you are studying was written more than a few decades ago, consult the *Oxford English Dictionary* to find out whether the meanings of any terms have shifted in the intervening period.

Good books are difficult to put down when you first read them. But a more leisurely second or third reading gives you the opportunity to make notes on those features you find significant. An index of characters and events is often useful, particularly when studying novels with a complex plot or time scheme. The main aim, however, should be to record your *responses* to the text. By all means note, for example, striking images. But be sure to add *why* you think them striking. Similarly, record any thoughts you may have on interesting comparisons with other texts, puzzling points of characterisation, even what you take to be aesthetic blemishes. The important thing is to annotate fully and adventurously. The most seemingly idiosyncratic comment may later lead to a crucial area of discussion which you would otherwise have overlooked. It helps to have a working copy of the text in which to mark up key passages and jot down marginal comments (although obviously these practices are taboo when working with library, borrowed or valuable copies!). But keep a fuller set of notes as well and organise these under appropriate headings.

Literature does not exist in an aesthetic vacuum, however, and you should try to find out as much as possible about the context of its production and reception. It is particularly important to read other works by the same author and writings by contemporaries. At this early stage, you may want to restrict your secondary reading to those standard reference works, such as biographies, which are widely available in public libraries. In the long run, however, it pays to read as wide a range of critical studies as possible.

Some students, and tutors, worry that such studies may stifle the development of any truly personal response. But this won't happen if you are alert to the danger and read critically. After all, you wouldn't passively accept what a stranger told you in conversation. The fact that a critic's views are in print does not necessarily make them any more authoritative (as a glance at the review pages of the *TLS* and *London Review of Books* will reveal). So question the views you find: 'Does this critic's interpretation agree with mine and where do we part company?' 'Can it be right to try and restrict this text's meanings to those found by its author or first audience?' 'Doesn't this passage treat a theatrical text as though it were a novel?' Often it is views which you reject which prove most valuable since they challenge you to articulate your own position with greater clarity. Be sure to keep careful notes on what the critic wrote, and your *reactions* to what the critic wrote.

Analyse the question

You cannot begin to answer a question until you understand what task it is you have been asked to perform. Recast the question in your own words and reconstruct the line of reasoning which lies behind it. Where there is a choice of topics, try to choose the one for which you are best prepared. It would, for example, be unwise to tackle 'How far do you agree that in *Paradise Lost* Milton transformed the epic models he inherited from ancient Greece and Rome?' without a working knowledge of Homer and Virgil (or *Paradise Lost* for that matter!). If you do not already know the works of these authors, the question should spur you on to read more widely — or discourage you from attempting it at all. The scope of an essay, however, is not always so obvious and you must remain alert to the implied demands of each question. How could you possibly 'Consider the view that *Wuthering Heights* transcends the conventions of the Gothic novel' without reference to at least some of those works which, the question suggests, have *not* transcended Gothic conventions?

When you have decided on a topic, analyse the terms of the question itself. Sometimes these self-evidently require careful definition: *tragedy* and *irony*, for example, are notoriously difficult concepts to pin down and you will probably need to consult a good dictionary of literary terms. Don't ignore, however, those seemingly innocuous phrases which often smuggle in significant assumptions. 'Does Macbeth lack the nobility of the true tragic hero?' obviously invites you to discuss nobility and the nature of the tragic hero. But what of 'lack' and 'true' — do they suggest that the play would be improved had Shakespeare depicted Macbeth in a different manner? or that tragedy is superior to other forms of drama? Remember that you are not expected meekly to agree with the assumptions implicit in the question. Some questions are deliberately provocative in order to stimulate an engaged response. Don't be afraid to take up the challenge.

Sketch out your preliminary ideas

'Which comes first, the evidence or the answer?' is one of those chicken and egg questions. How can you form a view without inspecting the evidence? But how can you know which evidence is relevant without some idea of what it is you are looking for? In practice the mind reviews evidence and formulates preliminary theories or hypotheses at one and the same time, although for the sake of clarity we have separated out the processes. Remember that these early ideas are only there to get you started. You *expect* to modify them in the light of the evidence you uncover. Your initial hypothesis may be an instinctive 'gut-reaction'. Or you may find that you prefer to 'sleep on the problem', allowing ideas to gell over a period of time. Don't worry in either case. The mind is quite capable of processing a vast amount of accumulated evidence, the product of previous reading and thought, and reaching sophisticated intuitive judgements. Eventually, however, you are going to have to think carefully through any ideas you arrive at by such intuitive processes. Are they logical? Do they take account of all the relevant factors? Do they fully answer the question set? Are there any obvious reasons to qualify or abandon them?

Assemble your evidence

Now is the time to return to the text and re-read it with the question and your working hypothesis firmly in mind. Many of the notes you have already made are likely to be useful, but assess the precise relevance of this material and make notes on any new evidence you discover. The important thing is to cast your net widely and take into account points which tend to undermine your case as well as those that support it. As always, ensure that your notes are full, accurate, and reflect your own critical judgements.

You may well need to go outside the text if you are to do full justice to the question. If you think that the 'Oedipus complex' may be relevant to an answer on *Hamlet* then read Freud and a balanced selection of those critics who have discussed the appropriateness of applying psychoanalytical theories to the interpretation of literature. Their views can most easily be tracked down by consulting the annotated bibliographies held by most major libraries (and don't be afraid to ask a librarian for help in finding and using these). Remember that you go to works of criticism not only to obtain information but to stimulate you into clarifying your own position. And that since life is short and many critical studies are long, judicious use of a book's index and/or contents list is not to be scorned. You can save yourself a great deal of future labour if you carefully record full bibliographic details at this stage.

Once you have collected the evidence, organise it coherently. Sort the detailed points into related groups and identify the quotations which support these. You must also assess the relative importance of each point, for in an essay of limited length it is essential to establish a firm set of priorities, exploring some ideas in depth while discarding or subordinating others.

Test your ideas

As we stressed earlier, a hypothesis is only a proposal, and one that you fully expect to modify. Review it with the evidence before you. Do you really still believe in it? It would be surprising if you did not want to modify it in some way. If you cannot see any problems, others may. Try discussing your ideas with friends and relatives. Raise them in class discussions. Your tutor is certain to welcome your initiative. The critical process is essentially collaborative and there is absolutely no reason why you should not listen to and benefit from the views of others. Similarly, you should feel free to test your ideas against the theories put forward in academic journals and books. But do not just borrow what you find. Critically analyse the views on offer and, where appropriate, integrate them into your own pattern of thought. You must, of course, give full acknowledgement to the sources of such views.

Do not despair if you find you have to abandon or modify significantly your initial position. The fact that you are prepared to do so is a mark of intellectual integrity. Dogmatism is never an academic virtue and many of the best essays explore the *process* of scholarly enquiry rather than simply record its results.

Plan your argument

Once you have more or less decided on your attitude to the question (for an answer is never really 'finalised') you have to present your case in the most persuasive manner. In order to do this you must avoid meandering from point to point and instead produce an organised argument — a structured flow of ideas and supporting evidence, leading logically to a conclusion which fully answers the question. Never begin to write until you have produced an outline of your argument.

You may find it easiest to begin by sketching out its main stage as a flow chart or some other form of visual presentation. But eventually you should produce a list of paragraph topics. The paragraph is the conventional written demarcation for a unit of thought and you can outline an argument quite simply by briefly summarising the substance of each paragraph and then checking that these points (you may remember your English teacher referring to them as topic sentences) really do follow a coherent order. Later you will be able to elaborate on each topic, illustrating and qualifying it as you go along. But you will find this far easier to do if you possess from the outset a clear map of where you are heading.

All questions require some form of an argument. Even so-called 'descriptive' questions *imply* the need for an argument. An adequate answer to the request to 'Outline the role of Iago in *Othello*' would do far more than simply list his appearances on stage. It would at the very least attempt to provide some *explanation* for his actions — is he, for example, a representative stage 'Machiavel'? an example of pure evil, 'motiveless malignity'? or a realistic study of a tormented personality reacting to identifiable social and psychological pressures?

Your conclusion ought to address the terms of the question. It may seem obvious, but 'how far do you agree', 'evaluate', 'consider', 'discuss', etc, are *not* interchangeable formulas and your conclusion must take account of the precise wording of the question. If asked 'How far do you agree?', the concluding paragraph of your essay really should state whether you are in complete agreement, total disagreement, or, more likely, partial agreement. Each preceding paragraph should have a clear justification for its existence and help to clarify the reasoning which underlies your conclusion. If you find that a paragraph serves no good purpose (perhaps merely summarising the plot), do not hesitate to discard it.

The arrangement of the paragraphs, the overall strategy of the argument, can vary. One possible pattern is dialectical: present the arguments in favour of one point of view (**thesis**); then turn to counter-arguments or to a rival interpretation (**antithesis**); finally evaluate the competing claims and arrive at your own conclusion (**synthesis**). You may, on the other hand, feel so convinced of the merits of one particular case that you wish to devote your entire essay to arguing that viewpoint persuasively (although it is always desirable to indicate, however briefly, that you are aware of alternative, if flawed, positions). As the essays contained in this volume demonstrate, there are many other possible strategies. Try to adopt the one which will most comfortably accommodate the demands of the question and allow you to express your thoughts with the greatest possible clarity.

Be careful, however, not to apply abstract formulas in a mechanical manner. It is true that you should be careful to define your terms. It is *not* true that every essay should begin with 'The dictionary defines *x* as . . .'. In fact, definitions are often best left until an appropriate moment for their introduction arrives. Similarly every essay should have a beginning, middle and end. But it does not follow that in your opening paragraph you should announce an intention to write an essay, or that in your concluding paragraph you need to signal an imminent desire to put down your pen. The old adages are often useful reminders of what constitutes good practice, but they must be interpreted intelligently.

Write out the essay

Once you have developed a coherent argument you should aim to communicate it in the most effective manner possible. Make certain you clearly identify yourself, and the question you are answering. Ideally, type your answer, or at least ensure your handwriting is legible and that you leave sufficient space for your tutor's comments. Careless presentation merely distracts from the force of your argument. Errors of grammar, syntax and spelling are far more serious. At best they are an irritating blemish, particularly in the work of a student who should be sensitive to the nuances of language. At worst, they seriously confuse the sense of your argument. If you are aware that you have stylistic problems of this kind, ask your tutor for advice at the earliest opportunity. Everyone, however, is liable to commit the occasional howler. The only remedy is to give yourself plenty of time in which to proof-read your manuscript (often reading it aloud is helpful) before submitting it.

Language, however, is not only an instrument of communication; it is also an instrument of thought. If you want to think clearly and precisely you should strive for a clear, precise prose style. Keep your sentences short and direct. Use modern, straightforward English wherever possible. Avoid repetition, clichés and wordiness. Beware of generalisations, simplifications, and overstatements. Orwell analysed the relationship between stylistic vice and muddled thought in his essay 'Politics and the English Language' (1946) — it remains essential reading (and is still readily available in volume 4 of the Penguin *Collected Essays, Journalism and Letters*). Generalisations, for example, are always dangerous. They are rarely true and tend to suppress the individuality of the texts in question. A remark such as 'Keats always employs sensuous language in his poetry' is not only fatuous (what, after all, does it mean? is *every* word he wrote equally 'sensuous'?) but tends to obscure interesting distinctions which could otherwise be made between, say, the descriptions in the 'Ode on a Grecian Urn' and those in 'To Autumn'.

The intelligent use of quotations can help you make your points with greater clarity. Don't sprinkle them throughout your essay without good reason. There is no need, for example, to use them to support uncontentious statements of fact. 'Macbeth murdered Duncan' does not require textual evidence (unless you wish to dispute Thurber's brilliant parody, 'The Great Macbeth Murder Mystery', which reveals Lady Macbeth's father as the culprit!). Quotations should be included, however, when they are necessary to support your case. The proposition that Macbeth's imaginative powers wither after he has killed his king would certainly require extensive quotation: you would almost certainly want to analyse key passages from both before and after the murder (perhaps his first and last soliloquies?). The key word here is 'analyse'. Quotations cannot make your points on their own. It is up to you to demonstrate their relevance and clearly explain to your readers *why* you want them to focus on the passage you have selected.

Most of the academic conventions which govern the presentation of essays are set out briefly in the style sheet below. The question of gender, however, requires fuller discussion. More than half the population of the world is female. Yet many writers still refer to an undifferentiated *man*kind, or write of the author and *his* public. We do not think that this convention has much to recommend it. At the very least, it runs the risk of introducing unintended sexist attitudes. And at times leads to such patent absurdities as 'Cleopatra's final speech asserts *man*'s true nobility'. With a little thought, you can normally find ways of expressing yourself which do not suggest that the typical author, critic or reader is male. Often you can simply use plural forms, which is probably a more elegant solution than relying on such awkward formulations as 's/he' or 'he and she'. You should also try to avoid distinguishing between male and female authors on the basis of forenames. Why *Jane* Austen and not *George* Byron? Refer to all authors by their last names unless there is some good reason not to. Where there may otherwise be confusion, say between T S and George Eliot, give the name in full when if first occurs and thereafter use the last name only.

Finally, keep your audience firmly in mind. Tutors and examiners are interested in understanding your conclusions and the processes by which you arrived at them. They are not interested in reading a potted version of a book they already know. **So don't pad out your work with plot summary.**

Hints for examinations

In an examination you should go through exactly the same processes as you would for the preparation of a term essay. The only difference lies in the fact that some of the stages will have had to take place before you enter the examination room. This should not bother you unduly. Examiners are bound to avoid the merely eccentric when they come to formulate papers and if you have read widely and thought deeply about the central issues raised by your set texts you can be confident you will have sufficient material to answer the majority of questions sensibly.

The fact that examinations impose strict time limits makes it *more*, rather than less, important that you plan carefully. There really is no point in floundering into an answer without any idea of where you are going, particularly when there will not be time to recover from the initial error.

Before you begin to answer any question at all, study the entire paper with care. Check that you understand the rubric and know how many questions you have to answer and whether any are compulsory. It may be comforting to spot a title you feel confident of answering well, but don't rush to tackle it: read *all* the questions before deciding which *combination* will allow you to display your abilities to the fullest advantage. Once you have made your choice, analyse each question, sketch out your ideas, assemble the evidence, review your initial hypothesis, plan your argument, *before* trying to write out an answer. And make notes at each stage: not only will these help you arrive at a sensible conclusion, but examiners are impressed by evidence of careful thought.

Plan your time as well as your answers. If you have practised writing timed essays as part of your revision, you should not find this too difficult. There can be a temptation to allocate extra time to the questions you know you can answer well; but this is always a short-sighted policy. You will find yourself left to face a question which would in any event have given you difficulty without even the time to give it serious thought. It is, moreover, easier to gain marks at the lower end of the scale than at the upper, and you will never compensate for one poor answer by further polishing two satisfactory answers. Try to leave some time at the end of the examination to re-read your answers and correct any obvious errors. If the worst comes to the worst and you run short of time, don't just keep writing until you are forced to break off in mid-paragraph. It is far better to provide for the examiner a set of notes which indicate the overall direction of your argument.

Good luck — but if you prepare for the examination conscientiously and tackle the paper in a methodical manner, you won't need it!

Short prose quotation incorporated in the text of the essay, within quotation marks.

deceiving Benedick and Beatrice into 'a mountain of affection th'one with th'other' (II.1.339–340). The basis of both plots is getting the victims to overhear other people speaking, as they think, honestly.

In fact, therefore, we are being presented with two types of deceit: that which is benevolent, like Don Pedro's or the Friar's seeking ultimately a harmony that can be expressed marriage, and that which is totally destructive, like Don The success of each type of deceit depends on a manipul language and an alteration of behaviour and appearances on the readiness of the victims to judge from what is pres their eyes and ears. Telling the two types apart may ult.

long verse quotation indented and introduced by a colon. No quotation marks are needed.

Three dots (ellipsis) indicate where words or es have been cut from ation or where (as here) quotation begins mid-sentence.

t is not as if any character is unaware of the difficult onship of appearance to reality: but nearly every one is led choose, of two alternatives, the wrong one. The best instance of this comes at the crisis of the play:

> HERO . . . seemed I ever otherwise to you?
> CLAUDIO Out of thee! Seeming! I will write against it.
> You seem to me as Dian in her orb,
> As chaste as is the bud ere it be blown;
> But you are more intemperate in your blood
> Than Venus, or those pampered animals
> That rage in savage sensuality.
>
>   (IV.1.53–59)

Line reference given directly after the quotation, in brackets.

Hero's innocent use of the word 'seemed' — not 'was' — gets Claudio on the raw, for it raises the issue of behaviour versus real nature that is the cause of his torment. It triggers remarkable anticipation of Othello's tortured animal im that highlights the emotional perception of the disju between appearance and what Claudio at this point beli be reality. He could not be more wrong; and he is wrong he trusted the suspect word of Don John and what he wa to see at Hero's window rather than the woman he chose to as his wife. ove must, as both Desdemona (*Othello*) and Cordelia (*King Lear*) know, depend on trust: it (or its lack) can never be *proved*. Claudio is given 'ocular proof' (*Othello* III.3.360) of Hero's apparent unchastity, just as Othello is of Desdemona's by Iago, a stage-managing and manipulating

book/play titles are given in italics. In a handwritten or typed manuscript this would appear as underlining: King Lear; Othello.

Short verse quotation incorporated in the text of the essay within quotation marks. If the quotation ran on into a second line of poetry, this would be indicated by a slash (/).

We have divided the following information into two sections. Part A describes those rules which it is essential to master no matter what kind of essay you are writing (including examination answers). Part B sets out some of the more detailed conventions which govern the documentation of essays.

PART A: LAYOUT

Titles of texts

Titles of published books, plays (of any length), long poems, pamphlets and periodicals (including newspapers and magazines), works of classical literature, and films should be underlined: e.g. <u>David Copperfield</u> (novel), <u>Twelfth Night</u> (play), <u>Paradise Lost</u> (long poem), <u>Critical Quarterly</u> (periodical), Horace's Ars Poetica (Classical work), Apocalypse Now (film).

Notice how important it is to distinguish between titles and other names. <u>Hamlet</u> is the play; Hamlet the prince. <u>Wuthering Heights</u> is the novel; Wuthering Heights the house. <u>Underlining</u> is the equivalent in handwritten or typed manuscripts of printed italics. So what normally appears in this volume as *Othello* would be written as <u>Othello</u> in your essay.

Titles of articles, essays, short stories, short poems, songs, chapters of books, speeches, and newspaper articles are enclosed in quotation marks; e.g. 'The Flea' (short poem), 'The Prussian Officer' (short story), 'Middleton's Chess Strategies' (article), 'Thatcher Defects!' (newspaper headline).

Exceptions: Underlining titles or placing them within quotation marks does not apply to sacred writings (e.g. Bible, Koran, Old Testament, Gospels) or parts of a book (e.g. Preface, Introduction, Appendix).

It is generally incorrect to place quotation marks around a title of a published book which you have underlined. The exception is 'titles within titles': e.g. <u>'Vanity Fair': A Critical Study</u> (title of a book about *Vanity Fair*).

Quotations

Short verse quotations of a single line or part of a line should be incorporated within quotation marks as part of the running text of your essay. Quotations of two or three lines of verse are treated in the same way, with line endings indicated by a slash(/). For example:

1 In <u>Julius Caesar</u>, Antony says of Brutus, 'This was the noblest Roman of them all'.
2 The opening of Antony's famous funeral oration, 'Friends, Romans, Countrymen, lend me your ears;/ I come to bury Caesar not to praise him', is a carefully controlled piece of rhetoric.

Longer verse quotations of more than three lines should be indented from the main body of the text and introduced in most cases with a colon. Do not enclose indented quotations within quotation marks. For example:

It is worth pausing to consider the reasons Brutus gives to justify his decision to assassinate Caesar:

> It must be by his death; and for my part,
> I know no personal cause to spurn at him,
> But for the general. He would be crowned.
> How might that change his nature, there's the question.

At first glance his rationale may appear logical . . .

Prose quotations of less than three lines should be incorporated in the text of the essay, within quotation marks. Longer prose quotations should be indented and the quotation marks omitted. For example:

1 Before his downfall, Caesar rules with an iron hand. His political opponents, the Tribunes Marullus and Flavius, are 'put to silence' for the trivial offence of 'pulling scarfs off Caesar's image'.
2 It is interesting to note the rhetorical structure of Brutus's Forum speech:

> Romans, countrymen, and lovers, hear me for my cause, and be silent that you may hear. Believe me for my honour, and have respect to mine honour that you may believe. Censure me in your wisdom, and awake your senses, that you may the better judge.

Tenses: When you are relating the events that occur within a work of fiction or describing the author's technique, it is the convention to use the present tense. Even though Orwell published *Animal Farm* in 1945, the book *describes* the animals' seizure of Manor Farm. Similarly, Macbeth always *murders* Duncan, despite the passage of time.

PART B: DOCUMENTATION

When quoting from verse of more than twenty lines, provide line references: e.g. In 'Upon Appleton House' Marvell's mower moves 'With whistling scythe and elbow strong' (l.393).

Quotations from plays should be identified by act, scene and line references: e.g. Prospero, in Shakespeare's The Tempest, refers to Caliban as 'A devil, a born devil' (IV.1.188). (i.e. Act 4. Scene 1. Line 188).

Quotations from prose works should provide a chapter reference and, where appropriate, a page reference.

Bibliographies should list full details of all sources consulted. The way in which they are presented varies, but one standard format is as follows:

1 Books and articles are listed in alphabetical order by the author's last name. Initials are placed after the surname.
2 If you are referring to a chapter or article within a larger work, you list it by reference to the author of the article or chapter, not the editor (although the editor is also named in the reference).
3 Give (in parentheses) the place and date of publication, e.g. (London, 1962). These details can be found within the book itself. Here are some examples:

> Brockbank, J.P., 'Shakespeare's Histories, English and Roman', in Ricks, C. (ed.) English Drama to 1710 (Sphere History of Literature in the English Language) (London, 1971).
>
> Gurr, A., 'Richard III and the Democratic Process', Essays in Criticism 24 (1974), pp. 39–47.
>
> Spivack, B., Shakespeare and the Allegory of Evil (New York, 1958).

Footnotes: In general, try to avoid using footnotes and build your references into the body of the essay wherever possible. When you do use them give the full bibliographic reference to a work in the first instance and then use a short title: e.g. See K. Smidt, Unconformities in Shakespeare's History Plays (London, 1982), pp. 43–47 becomes Smidt (pp. 43–47) thereafter. Do not use terms such as 'ibid.' or 'op. cit.' unless you are absolutely sure of their meaning.

There is a principle behind all this seeming pedantry. The reader ought to be able to find and check your references and quotations as quickly and easily as possible. Give additional information, such as canto or volume number whenever you think it will assist your reader.

SUGGESTIONS FOR FURTHER READING

Dollimore, Jonathan, 'Transgression and Surveillance in *Measure for Measure*', in Dollimore, Jonathan, and Sinfield, Alan (eds), *Political Shakespeare* (Manchester, 1985), pp. 72–87

Goldberg, Jonathan, *James I and the Politics of Literature* (London, 1983)

Hawkins, Harriet, *Measure for Measure: Harvester New Critical Introduction to Shakespeare* (London, 1987)

Jardine, Lisa, *Still Harping on Daughters* (London, 1983)

Ricks, Christopher (ed.) *English Drama to 1710*, Sphere History of Literature in the English Language (London, 1971)

Rose, Jacqueline, 'Sexuality in the Reading of Shakespeare: *Hamlet* and *Measure for Measure*', in Drakakis, John (ed.), *Alternative Shakespeares* (1985), pp. 95–118

Schanzer, Ernest, *The Problem Plays of Shakespeare* (London, 1963)

Stead, C K (ed.), *Measure for Measure: A Casebook* (London, 1971)

Watts, Cedric, *Measure for Measure: A Critical Study* (Harmondsworth, 1986)

Wells, Stanley (ed.), *The Cambridge Companion to Shakespeare Studies* (Cambridge, 1986)

Longman Group UK Limited
Longman House, Burnt Mill, Harlow, Essex, CM20 2JE, England
and Associated Companies throughout the World.

First published 1991
ISBN 0 582 07576 9

Set in 10/12 pt Century Schoolbook, Linotron 202
Printed in Great Britain by Bell and Bain Ltd., Glasgow

Acknowledgement
The editors would like to thank Zachary Leader for his assistance with
the style sheet.